AF872055

# ON THE CONTENT AND OBJECT OF PRESENTATIONS

MELBOURNE INTERNATIONAL PHILOSOPHY SERIES

VOLUME 4

# ON THE CONTENT AND OBJECT OF PRESENTATIONS

*by*

DR. KASIMIR TWARDOWSKI

*translated by*

R. GROSSMANN

---



Communications to be addressed to the Editor, c/o Philosophy Department, University of Melbourne, Parkville, 3052, Victoria, Australia.

# ON THE CONTENT AND OBJECT OF PRESENTATIONS

## A PSYCHOLOGICAL INVESTIGATION

*by*

Dr. KASIMIR TWARDOWSKI

*translated and with an introduction by*

R. GROSSMANN

MARTINUS NIJHOFF - THE HAGUE - 1977

ISBN-13: 978-90-247-1926-6 e-ISBN-13: 978-94-010-1050-4
DOI: 10.1007/978-94-010-1050-4

# TABLE OF CONTENTS

# INTRODUCTION

Twardowski's little book – of which I here offer a translation – is one of the most remarkable works in the history of modern philosophy. It is concise, clear, and – in Findlay's words – "amazingly rich in ideas."[1] It is therefore a paradigm of what some contemporary philosophers approvingly call "analytic philosophy." But Twardowski's book is also of considerable historical significance. His views reflect Brentano's earlier position and thus shed some light on this stage of Brentano's philosophy. Furthermore, they form a link between this stage, on the one hand, and those two grandiose attempts to propagate rationalism in an age of science, on the other hand, which are known as Meinong's theory of entities and Husserl's phenomenology. Twardowski's views thus point to the future and introduce many of the problems which, through the influence of Meinong, Husserl, Russell, and Moore, have become standard fare in contemporary philosophy. In this introduction, I shall call attention to the close connection between some of Twardowski's main ideas and the corresponding thoughts of these four philosophers.

## I. IDEAS AND THEIR INTENTIONS

Twardowski's main contention is clear. He claims that we must distinguish between the act, the content, and the object of a presentation. The crucial German term is '*Vorstellung.*' This term has a corresponding verb and allows for such expressions as '*das Vorgestellte.*' From a purely philosophical point of view, the best translation of '*Vorstellung*' is, in my opinion, the word 'idea.' But there is no corresponding verb in English, nor can we easily translate '*das Vorgestellte.*' I have therefore followed the common practice and translated '*Vorstellung,*' not by 'idea,' but rather by 'presentation.' But I have done so with some mis-

[1] See J. N. Findlay, *Meinong's Theory of Objects and Values*, 2d ed. (Oxford, 1963), p. 8.

givings; for this translation destroys some of the philosophic flavor of the text. It fails to stress that the *Vorstellungen* of the German (Kantian) tradition are the ideas of the British (Lockean) tradition.

The case is straightforward for the other two terms '*Inhalt*' and '*Gegenstand*.' I translate them as 'content' and 'object,' respectively. But this is not the terminology which I shall use in the rest of this introduction. Here my interests are purely philosophical, and I shall therefore feel free to use a terminology which best suits these interests. A presentation, as Twardowski thinks of it, is a mental act which has two parts. One of these parts – the *kind* (of act), if you wish – determines that the act in question is a presentation rather than, say, a judgment or a desire. The second part of the act is the so-called *content*. This content determines what particular object the presentation brings before the mind. Strictly speaking, therefore, it is not the whole act of presentation, but only the content, which is "of" a certain object. This is the reason why I shall in this introduction identify the content of a presentation with an idea. Contents of presentations are, I suggest, the ideas (notions, concepts) of the British tradition. A presentation, in the sense of mental act, coincides with a mental act of *having* an idea. The object of a presentation is that entity of which the respective idea is an idea. In brief, I shall speak of an idea, the act of having an idea, and the object of an idea where Twardowski speaks of the content of a presentation, the act of presentation, and the object of a presentation, respectively.

Twardowski distinguishes between two main kinds of ideas, namely, individual ideas (ideas of individual things) and general ideas (concepts). This distinction reflects the Kantian division of ideas into intuitions (*Anschauungen*) and concepts (*Begriffe*). While it is clear that an individual idea is the idea of an individual thing, it is not equally clear what it is that a concept is a concept of. Twardowski insists that a concept does not intend a plurality of individual things; the concept (of) green, for example, does not intend a plurality of individual green things. Thus what a concept intends is not the same as what falls under a concept. In this respect, Twardowski differs from most of his contemporaries and is, I think, on the side of the angels. But Twardowski does not clearly state what kind of entity a concept does intend. If I understand him correctly, he does not hold, as I would, that a concept intends a property. Instead, he seems to believe that it intends a "group of constituents" of individual things. An individual thing is, in Twardowski's view, a *complex* ("collection," "bundle") of particularized properties or, as I shall say, of *instances*. Two individual things which have precisely the same shade of color thus contain, as constituents, two instances of this color. These two instances, although they are not identical or the same, stand in the relation of color-similarity. A concept, then, intends a group of instances, namely, a group of instances which is determined by a certain equivalence relation.

The word 'object,' as used by Brentano's students, is systematically ambiguous. An object is whatever a mental act may put before a mind. In this sense, anything that can be before a mind, no matter what kind of entity it is, is called an object. But the word 'object' is also used for a certain kind of entity, namely, for individual things. Now, as long as one holds, like Brentano, that all the entities there are, are individual things, no terminological problem need arise. But if one admits – like Meinong and Husserl – that there are other categories, for example, states of affairs, then one must change one's terminology. I shall speak of the *intention* of a mental act whenever I wish to leave open what kind of entity the mental act intends. For example, when Meinong calls his newly discovered field of inquiry "Gegenstandstheorie," he does not mean to talk about a theory of individual things. Rather, what he has in mind is a general theory of *intentions*, a theory of *entities*.

Twardowski thus holds that the intentions of individual ideas are objects, while the intentions of concepts are groups of objects, namely, objects which are parts of other objects. Does this mean that he thinks of a *group* of objects as another object? I do not know the answer. Since I believe that a group (set, class) of individual things is not an individual thing, I am not sure that his view of the intentions of concepts is acceptable. But be that as it may, let us turn from presentations to judgments.

Twardowski maintains that the threefold distinction between act, content, and object also applies to judgments. A judgment, just like a presentation, consists of two parts, a *kind* and a *content*. The kind is, of course, an instance of the property of being a judgment rather than of the property of being a presentation. So far the parallel between judgment and presentation is perfect. But then Twardowski says something very startling about the content of a judgment, namely, that the content of a judgment is the *existence* of the object which is affirmed or denied by means of the judgment. This comes as quite a surprise, because one expects something more like the following view instead. Just as objects have their mental pictures in the form of ideas, so the intentions of judgments have their mental counterparts in the form of what we may call judgments.[2] And just as we must distinguish between an idea, the act of having this idea, and the intention of the idea, so we must distinguish between a judgment, the act of making the judgment, and the intention of the judgment. Judgments, as distinguished from acts of making judgments, would then consist of ideas.

Twardowski does not extend the content-object distinction in this obvious way to judgments because he embraces Brentano's early theory of judgment.[3] According to this theory, every judgment is an affirmation or a denial of the existence of an object. Hence there is no room in this theory for special contents and special intentions of judgments. Every judgment merely affirms or denies an individual thing which is presented to the mind through an idea. The content of a judgment simply coincides with the content of the underlying presentation, that is, with the idea which presents the object in question to the mind. And the intention of the judgment simply coincides with the intention of the underlying presentation, that is, with the object of the idea in question. According to this theory of judgment, there is only one kind of "inner picture" which sets things before the mind, namely, ideas; and there is only one kind of "outer intention" which is brought before the mind, namely, objects. But a mind may adopt, as it were, different attitudes toward these objects: they can be affirmed or denied, and they can be desired or abhorred. This is the gist of Brentano's famous doctrine that every mental act either is a presentation or rests on a presentation.[4] Twardowski, we noted, adds a peculiar twist to Brentano's theory by identifying the content of a judgment, not with the content of the underlying presentation, but with the existence of the object judged.[5] I do not think that this is an improvement on Brentano's theory; for I fail to understand how the existence of an object can somehow be an "inner picture" of the intention of a judgment, in

[2] Since a so-called judgment and an assumption may have the same content, the same mental counterpart to the judged or assumed state of affairs, one could say that they involve the same *thought*. In this fashion, contents of presentations, that is, ideas, would be contrasted with contents of propositional mental acts, that is, thoughts.

[3] See Brentano's defense of this theory in the selection from the *Psychologie vom empirischen Standpunkt* which appears translated in *Realism and the Background of Phenomenology*, R. M. Chisholm ed. (New York and London, 1960); and also J. Srzednicki, *Franz Brentano's Analysis of Truth* (The Hague, 1965).

[4] Compare Husserl's painstaking analysis of this doctrine in chapters three and four of the fifth investigation of his *Logical Investigations*, 2d ed., translated by J. N. Findlay (New York, 1970).

[5] In a letter to Meinong, Twardowski says that he plans to write a book on judgments which is based on this identification. See *Philosophenbriefe. Aus der wissenschaftlichen Korrespondenz von Alexius Meinong*, Rudolf Kindinger ed. (Graz, 1965), pp. 143–144.

analogy to the way in which the content of a presentation is an "inner picture" of the object presented.

Both Meinong and Husserl eventually abandon Brentano's early theory of judgment. They discover the category of states of affairs. Judgments (and other "propositional" acts like assumptions) are said to intend states of affairs rather than objects. This new view of judgments invites an extension of Twardowski's threefold distinction along the lines indicated a moment ago. But such an extension also leads to new problems. Twardowski faces the problem of how to analyze the fact that there are ideas of nonexistent objects, for example, of the golden mountain and of the round square. With the advent of states of affairs, there arises also the problem of how to analyze the fact that there are false beliefs, that is, beliefs in nonexistent states of affairs. Let us take a look at both of these problems simultaneously under the heading of the problem of nonexistent intentions.

## 2. THE PROBLEM OF NONEXISTENT INTENTIONS

Meinong's theory of entities and Husserl's phenomenology rest on the same two basic theses. According to the first thesis, every mental act has an intention; the second thesis states that intentions have properties and stand in relations irrespective of their ontological status. The theory of entities is simply the theory of intentions; and so, of course, is phenomenology. But there could be no theory of intentions in general unless the second thesis is true. Twardowski, I wish to point out, defends both of these theses.

Every idea, Twardowski maintains, has an object. Consider, for example, the idea of a round square. Some philosophers thought that this idea has no object. That they were mistaken can be seen, according to Twardowski, from the fact that the entity whose existence one denies because it has inconsistent properties is, not the idea of a round square, but a round square itself. He is arguing, in other words, that if one denies the existence of something, then this something must be before the mind. Moreover, this something cannot be an idea, since the idea most assuredly does not have the (contradictory) properties which the something has. Twardowski thus argues that since the round square *is* round and square, while the idea of it is neither, the round square rather than the idea of it must be before the mind. He uses the second thesis in order to prove the first.

But if it is true that every idea has an object, how did the mistaken notion gain acceptance that there are "objectless" ideas? Twardowski thinks that one confused the nonexistence of an object with its not being presented. He insists that we must distinguish between two very different questions. The first question is: Does a given idea intend something? The second question is: Does it intend an entity that has being?[6] The answer to the first question is always affirmative: all ideas intend something. But the answer to the second question may or may not be affirmative, since some intentions have no being. Therefore, the fact that an idea has an object does not imply that this object has being. Twardowski holds, furthermore, that there is a certain indefinable relation between every idea and its object. I shall call this relation "the intentional nexus." In terms of this nexus, Twardowski's view can then be described as follows. We must distinguish between the question of whether or not the intentional nexus holds between an idea and its object, on the one hand, and the question of whether the object has being, on the other. Every idea is related by means of the intentional nexus to "its" object, but it does not automatically follow that this object has being. Twardowski thus implies that the intentional nexus can hold between a mental entity which has being, the content, and something which has no ontological status whatsoever, the object. He maintains, in other words, that there is at least one "extraordinary" relation which spans the realm of being and the realm of nonbeing. I shall call this "Twardowski's basic assumption." His solution of the problem of nonexistent objects rests on this basic assumption.

Twardowski's basic assumption can easily be extended to states of affairs. One merely has to assume that the same intentional nexus also connects judgments (thoughts) with states of affairs. Just as this nexus connects on some occasions an existent idea with an object which has no ontological status whatsoever, so it may also connect an existent judgment with a state of affairs which has no being. A belief, for example, is true if and only if it intends a fact, that is, a subsistent state of affairs. A belief is false, on the other hand, if and only if it intends a state of affairs which does not even subsist, that is, which has no being at all. We may, therefore, speak in general of Twardowski's solution of the problem of nonexistent intentions. It rests on an extension of Twardowski's basic assumption, namely, on the assumption that the

[6] The philosophers whom I mention in this introduction distinguish usually between existence and subsistence. Existents are those entities which have being in space and/or time. Subsistents have being, too, but are not localized. States of affairs, for example, are usually said to subsist, if they are facts. The state of affairs that the earth is flat, on the other hand, is said to have no being at all.

intentional nexus can connect various sorts of mental contents with various kinds of intentions, irrespective of whether or not these intentions have being.[7]

If we assume that intentionality consists in the intentional nexus, as I shall throughout this introduction, then there seems to be only one alternative to Twardowski's solution of the problem of nonexistent intentions.[8] I shall call this alternative "Russell's solution" because it was once defended by Russell.[9] The main idea of Russell's solution is that false beliefs must intend states of affairs which have the same ontolotical status as facts. Since the intentions of true beliefs are said to subsist, it follows that the states of affairs intended by false beliefs subsist, too. But there is an "objective" difference between true and false belief. Even though the intentions of true and false beliefs equally subsist, the intentions of true beliefs have a certain characteristic which those of false beliefs lack, and conversely. Russell says that the states of affairs intended by true beliefs have the characteristic of being true, while those intended by false beliefs have the characteristic of being false.

There are a number of variations of Russell's solution. What distinguishes among these versions is the nature of the characteristic which divides states of affairs into facts and non-facts. For example, Frege holds that while true beliefs intend states of affairs (more accurately, thoughts) which are somehow connected with the object *true*, false beliefs intend states of affairs which are somehow connected with the object *false*.[10] Other variations do not ascribe full subsistence to non-factual states of affairs, but insist nevertheless that even non-factual states of affairs have some kind of being. Bergmann, for example, maintains that facts exist in the mode of possibility.[11] What all of these versions have in common, however, is Russell's rejection of Twardowski's basic assumption.

Russell argues, against Twardowski's basic assumption, that a false

[7] I have described and defended this view in greater detail in my *The Structure of Mind* (Madison and Milwaukee, 1965).

[8] There are philosophers, of course, who do not share this assumption. At one point, Brentano rejected it and then invented the so-called "adverbial analysis" of intentionality. See on this point, for example, my article "Acts and Relations in Brentano," *Analysis*, 21 (1960), 1–5.

[9] See Russell's "Meinong's Theory of Complexes and Assumptions," *Mind*, 13 (1904), 204–219, 336–354, and 509–524.

[10] See Frege's "On Sense and Reference," in *Translations from the Philosophical Writings of Gottlob Frege* (Oxford, 1960).

[11] See Bergmann's *Realism. A Critique of Brentano and Meinong* (Madison, Milwaukee, and London, 1967).

belief intends a state of affairs just as much as a true belief and that, therefore, the state of affairs intended by a false belief must subsist.[12] Twardowski, of course, would agree with the first part of this assertion. But he would point out that the second part does not follow from the first, since the intentional nexus is of a peculiar sort. Russell's argument, then, merely comes down to whether or not there is such a peculiar relation: Russell assumes that there is no such nexus, while Twardowski thinks that there is. But Russell adds another argument.[13] It is a fact that the golden mountain has no being. Hence there subsists the state of affairs that the golden mountain has no being. But this state of affairs is quite obviously a complex entity, a whole, which consists of certain entities. Among the constituents of this complex entity, moreover, is the golden mountain. Now, it is a fundamental principle that a whole cannot have being unless all of its parts have being. Hence, we are forced to conclude that the golden mountain has being, since it is a constituent of a state of affairs which has being. We must therefore reject Twardowski's view that the golden mountain has no being. Similarly, for non-factual states of affairs: they, too, can occur as constituents of complex factual states of affairs and, therefore, must subsist. For example, the complex state of affairs *P or Q* subsists, even if *P* is a fact and *Q* is not a fact. Since *Q* is then a constituent of a subsistent, it must itself subsist.

Meinong discusses this argument from the being of complexes to the being of their constituents, but arrives at a different conclusion.[14] After a certain amount of vacillation, he rejects the principle about the being of wholes and their parts. He maintains that since the golden mountain does not exist, and since it is a fact that it does not exist, a whole may have being (subsistence, in this case), even if one of its parts has no being. And this immediately implies that the part-whole relation is as "peculiar" as the intentional nexus. The former relation, too, must be capable of holding between an entity which has no being and an entity which has being. Similarly, for connectives between states of affairs. The connective *or* (the relation, not the word) can hold between a fact and a state of affairs which has no being. What Russell's argument shows is that we cannot stop with just one peculiar relation, the intentional nexus, if we admit that states of affairs are complex entities and

[12] See, for example, "Meinong's Theory of Complexes and Assumptions," p. 510, and p. 515.
[13] See Russell's "Meinong's Theory of Complexes and Assumptions," p. 511.
[14] See the translation of Meinong's paper "Ueber Gegenstandstheorie" in *Realism and the Background of Phenomenology*.

if we decline to ascribe ontological status to such entities as the golden mountain, the round square, and non-factual states of affairs. What Russell's argument shows is that Twardowski's basic assumption soon leads to the appearance of further "peculiar" relations.

Twardowski's solution of the problem of nonexistent intentions consists in the acceptance of what may be thought to be peculiar relations, but it does agree with commonsense that such entities as the golden mountain, the round square, and non-factual states of affairs, have no being. Russell's solution, on the other hand, consists in a rejection of those peculiar relations, but does not agree with commonsense in regard to the being of the golden mountain, the round square, and non-factual states of affairs. The dialectic of the problem seems to offer nothing better than two horns of a dilemma: either accept the existence of a number of peculiar relations, or else make yourself believe that what has no being does have being after all. Russell, as we saw, chose at first the second horn. But his robust sense of reality revolted against the being of the round square. His famous theory of descriptions can be viewed as an attempt to escape from the first horn without having to embrace the second.[15] It tries to reconcile two requirements: there must be no peculiar part-whole relation and there must be no round square and the like.

From this point of view, Russell's theory of descriptions attempts to show that a state of affairs like *The round square does not exist* does not contain a part or constituent which is represented by the expression 'the round square.' Since it does not contain such a part, it follows that we are not forced to ascribe being to this part even though the whole state of affairs has being and even though the fundamental principle of the being of wholes and parts holds.

In order to show that the round square is not a part of the state of affairs that the round square does not exist, Russell gives a "contextual definition" of sentences with definite descriptions in terms of the existential quantifier and a so-called uniqueness clause. He claims that the state of affairs represented by a sentence with a definite description is *more perspicuously* represented by a second sentence which does not contain a definite description. Therefore, the constituents of this state of affairs are more perspicuously indicated by the second sentence. And this second sentence shows that the state of affairs in question does not contain a part which corresponds to the definite description. Instead, it contains certain properties. For example, the state of affairs that the

[15] See Russell's "On Denoting," *Mind*, 14 (1905), 479–493.

round square does not exist contains, among other entities, the properties *round* and *square*.

It is clear that Russell must maintain that the sentence with the definite description is merely another expression for the state of affairs which is also, but more perspicuously, represented by the sentence with the existential quantifier and the uniqueness clause. Meinong, it should be pointed out, does not object to Russell's theory as such. Rather, he contends that this particular claim is false. The states of affairs represented by the two sentences – the sentence with the definite description and the sentence with the existential quantifier and the uniqueness clause – are in his view not the *same*, but are merely *equivalent*. While it is true, as Russell claims, that the second sentence does not represent a state of affairs which contains as a part an entity which is represented by the expression 'the round square,' the first sentence nevertheless does represent such a state of affairs. And since this latter state of affairs does contain the entity *the round square*, Russell has not escaped, in Meinong's view, from the horns of the dilemma.

I shall not try to argue here whether or not Meinong is right.[16] Let us turn instead to another problem with Russell's attempt to escape from the dilemma. Even if we set aside Meinong's objection, the dilemma has only been avoided for such entities as the round square and the golden mountain, but it has not been avoided for non-factual states of affairs. Russell is still faced with the question what the ontological status is of the intentions of false beliefs. Consider the state of affairs that the golden mountain exists. This state of affairs, we shall grant, does not contain a golden mountain. But does it have any being? Russell argues later on that it has no being, but he also sticks to his rejection of Twardowski's basic assumption.[17] He holds that in the case of a true belief, there subsists a certain complex entity, a fact, which is intended by the belief. When a belief is false, though, then there is no such complex entity before the mind; for, if such an entity were before the mind, then it would have to subsist and the belief would not be false, contrary to our assumption. But it is not the case that there is nothing at all before the mind when the belief is false, that the mind is completely blank, so to speak. Rather, the mind is in such a case somehow multiply related to certain entities which would be constitu-

[16] For a detailed discussion of this point see my "Meinong's Doctrine of the *Aussersein* of the Pure Object," *Nous*, 8 (1974), 67–81.

[17] See Russell's "On the Nature of Truth," *Proceedings of the Aristotelian Society* (1906–1907), 28–49, pp. 46–47; and also his "The Philosophy of Logical Atomism," in *Logic and Knowledge*, Robert Charles Marsh ed. (London, 1966).

ents of a state of affairs if there were such a state of affairs. For example, if someone believes mistakenly that Desdemona loves Cassio, then his mind is somehow related to Desdemona, to Cassio, and to a relation of loving, but it is not related to the state of affairs that Desdemona loves Cassio, because there is no such state of affairs. I do not think that this way out of the dilemma will do. Russell's new analysis fails to account for the difference between believing mistakenly that Desdemona loves Cassio and believing mistakenly – as we shall assume, for the sake of the argument – that Cassio loves Desdemona. In either case, the mind would somehow be related separately to the three entities mentioned earlier. Yet it is obvious that the two beliefs are beliefs in very different things. Moreover, it simply flies in the face of commonsense to assert that the false belief that Desdemona loves Cassio consists entirely in "thinking" separately of Desdemona, Cassio, and loving, without having any state of affairs before the mind. To put it differently, if this state of affairs were not before the mind, then there would simply be no belief that Desdemona loves Cassio and, hence, we could not have a false belief.

It is ironic that in the minds of contemporary philosophers Russell is the ontologically moderate miser and Meinong is the spendthrift. Russell's first response to the problem of nonexistent intentions, as we noted, was to confer being of some sort on all of these entities. This, of course, would be the response of the ontological spendthrift. Meinong, on the other hand, follows in the footsteps of Twardowski and denies that such entities as the golden mountain and the round square have being. Meinong's infamous doctrine of the "*Aussersein*" of the pure object rests on Twardowski's basic assumption. Perhaps it is not too late to convince some contemporary philosophers that Meinong did not hold that the round square has some kind of being.

It is true, however, that Meinong flirted at times with Russell's wholesale admission of nonexistent intentions into the realm of being. But his view on *Aussersein* is designed specifically to avoid this horn of the main dilemma.[18] Compare the golden mountain $G$ with a certain existing mountain $M$. According to Meinong's general assay of individual things, each one of these two entities consists of certain properties, each one is, as I shall say, a complex of properties.[19] Meinong's doctrine

[18] Compare Meinong's paper "Ueber Gegenstandstheorie" and also his book *Ueber Annahmen*, 2d ed. (Leipzig, 1910), pp. 79–80. For a discussion of Meinong's view see my paper mentioned in footnote 16 and my book *Meinong* (London and Boston, 1974), chapter 6.

[19] A complex of properties must not be confused with a complex property, as I shall emphasize presently.

of the *Aussersein* of the pure object, as I understand it, contains two main ideas. The first idea, an idea which Meinong introduces into the dialectic of nonexistent objects, is that being is never a constituent of an individual thing.[20] The golden mountain, for example, consists of such properties as that of being golden and that of being a mountain, but it does not contain any form of being as a constituent. Nor does the mountain *M*, even though we have assumed that it exists, contain existence. Existence is not one of the constituents of the complex which is the mountain *M*. The second idea is simply Twardowski's basic assumption, namely, that an idea can intend an object which has no being.

But if the fact that the mountain *M* exists is not to be viewed as the fact that the complex entity *M* somehow contains existence, how is it to be analyzed? Meinong answers that being is always a matter of objectives, that is, of states of affairs. Since *M* exists, he maintains, there subsists a certain state of affairs, *SM*, to the effect that *M* exists. Since the golden mountain *G* does not exist, there subsists a certain state of affairs, *not-SG*, to the effect that *G* does not exist. But in this case, there subsists no state of affairs to the effect that *G* exists. In short, while there is the state of affairs that *M* exists, there is no corresponding state of affairs that *G* exists.

It is clear that Meinong's doctrine of the *Aussersein* of the pure object does not advance the dialectic of the problem of nonexistent intentions very much. Just as in the case of Russell's theory of definite descriptions – to which Meinong's doctrine is a respectable alternative – there remains the most important problem of how to deal with non-factual states of affairs. Assume that someone mistakenly believes that the golden mountain exists. In this case, there is a certain state of affairs, *SG*, before his mind. This state of affairs does not subsist. Yet it is intended by a belief. Meinong, although he is not always too clear about this matter, seems to hold that Twardowski's basic assumption also holds for states of affairs. Thus he embraces the first horn of the basic dilemma. Notice that there is a certain asymmetry between Meinong's treatment of individual things and his treatment of states of affairs. While there is the notion that the pure object does not contain being, the same is not true of objectives. To say of an object that it

[20] Compare this analysis with Moore's early view, according to which existence is an ingredient in objects, as contained in his "The Nature of Judgment," *Mind*, 8 (1899), 176–193. For a discussion of Moore's early ontology see H. Hochberg, "Moore's Ontology and Non-natural Properties," in *Studies in the Philosophy of G. E. Moore*, E. D. Klemke ed. (Chicago, 1969).

exists, is not at all like saying of an object that it has some property; it is not to say that the object contains existence as it contains its properties. Rather, it is to say of the object that there subsists a certain objective for it, namely, the existence of the object. But this kind of analysis cannot be given for the subsistence of objectives. To say of an objective that it subsists is not to say of it that there subsists a certain further objective for it, namely the subsistence of the first objective. Meinong thinks that this analysis leads to an objectionable infinite regress. He holds, therefore, that the first objective must somehow contain subsistence in itself, it must somehow contain both the object whose existence it is as well as existence (or some other kind of being). Thus there can be no "pure" objectives analogously to "pure" objects. We shall see in the next section that Meinong's view on non-factual states of affairs encounters severe difficulty.

To sum up, neither Russell nor Meinong escapes from the horns of the basic dilemma in regard to false beliefs. But while Meinong later takes Twardowski's horn, Russell seeks a way out by propounding his multiple relation theory of belief. As I pointed out, I do not think that Russell's theory has anything to recommend it. If so, then there is really only one alternative to Twardowski's basic assumption and that is, of course, Russell's early view that all states of affairs have being. If there is no way out, as I am claiming, then we must decide between the two views, we must try to show that we are not confronted with a dilemma after all because one of the two alternatives, though they looked equally unacceptable, is acceptable after all. I think that Twardowski's solution is the correct one, but I cannot argue this case here in detail. However, I shall briefly consider one argument against it which, in my view, is not sound. And I shall also mention one consideration that seems to speak against the Russellian alternative.

It is sometimes said that the intentional relation could not possibly hold between an existent and a non-existent because this would mean that it would have to be a relation with only one term, and a one-term relation is simply an absurdity. An entity with just one term, in the sense in question, would have to be a property, if anything at all, but could not possibly be a relation. In short, it is said that the very notion of a relation requires it to have more than one existent term. But this argument seems to rest on an equivocation. The notion of a relation with just one term is indeed absurd; a relation with just one term would be an ontological absurdity. But when we assert that the intentional relation can connect an idea with a nonexistent object, we do not imply that it is such a one-term relation and, hence, an absurdity. The intentional nexus is a two-term relation. But, and this is the crux of the matter, the entities which stand in this two-term relation need not both exist. We must distinguish between the terms of a relation, the number of terms which a relation has, on the one hand, and the entities which stand in this relation, on the other. This distinction is already forced upon us when we consider the relation of identity or sameness. Meinong, among other philosophers, argues at one point that such a relation is an absurdity, and he argues against it along the very same lines as our critic of the intentional nexus as defended by Twardowski.[21] And here, too, our answer consists in making the distinction just indicated between term and entity. The identity relation is a two-term relation; no doubt about that. But when it holds, then there is just one entity that occurs in the positions of both terms.[22]

According to Russell's alternative, every state of affairs has being, but not every state of affairs has the characteristic of being, let us say, factual. It follows that to say of a state of affairs $S$ that it is factual is not to say that the state of affairs $T$, to the effect that $S$ is factual, has being. Otherwise, the distinction between true and false beliefs would collapse. The two states of affairs $S$ and $T$ cannot even be equivalent. In general, the state of affairs that a certain entity $R$ has the characteristic $C$ is not equivalent to the state of affairs that $E$'s having $C$ has being. Predication and being part ways, so to speak. It is this parting of ways which I find implausible. If there is the state of affairs *A is C*, if there is this complex entity, then $A$ must be $C$. I cannot see how it could be otherwise. This, of course, is Russell's later consideration, which leads him to abandon his earlier view. But while it suggests to him the multiple relation theory of belief, it suggests to me, for reasons which I have indicated, that Twardowski's analysis is correct.

## 3. THE PROPERTIES OF NONEXISTENT OBJECTS

So far we have discussed the first of the two theses which form the cornerstones of the theory of entities and of phenomenology, namely, the proposition that every mental act has an intention. Let us now turn to the second thesis. According to this proposition, nonexistent objects have properties and stand in relations just as do existent objects. As

[21] See Meinong's *Hume Studien* II: *Zur Relationstheorie*, 1882, in *Gesammelte Abhandlungen*, vol. 2 (Leipzig, 1913), p. 130.

[22] Russell gives essentially the same answer in his *The Principle of Mathematics*, 2d ed. (London, 1937), p. 64.

I said earlier, this thesis, too, goes back to Twardowski; and it is again Russell who holds an opposing view.

Meinong, following in Twardowski's footsteps, maintains that the golden mountain is golden and that the round square is both round and square. Russell, in his review of the *Untersuchungen*, raises two main objections against this claim. Before we take a look at these objections, let us ask how Twardowski, Meinong, and Husserl may have arrived at the rather peculiar view in question.

An ordinary perceptual object – a chair, for example – is in Twardowski's view (as well as in Meinong's and Husserl's) a complex entity consisting of a number of instances of properties (and relations). It is, to use Berkeley's term, a *collection* of particularized properties. Twardowski does not tell us how the properties become particularized, but if we take a hint from Meinong, then we may guess that they are particularized because they are associated with certain places and moments.[23] Space and time are, so to speak, the forms of individuation. At any rate, according to Twardowski's view, to say of an individual thing that it has a certain property is to say of it that it contains as a *constituent* a certain instance. The relationship between an individual thing and its properties is neither exemplification nor participation, but is the whole-part relation.

Turn now to the golden mountain. It is obvious that the golden mountain cannot be individuated by being localized in space and time. Hence it must consist, not of instances of properties, but of properties. Twardowski, I must quickly add, does not quite say all this, but I think that we may again take a cue from Meinong's work. Thus, while a real mountain is a complex of instances, the golden mountain turns out to be a complex of properties. But this conception of individual things, and especially of nonexistent individuals, easily invites a confusion between the *complex of properties* (or of instances) which is the individual thing and the corresponding *complex property* (complex instance). For example, we may ask how the golden mountain differs from the complex property of being golden and a mountain, since both of these entities presumably consist of the same properties; they are both conceived of as wholes which have the same properties as parts. To put the matter differently, consider, on the one hand, the relationship between an individual thing and its properties and, on the other, the relationship between a complex property and the properties of which it consists If,

[23] See *Gesammelte Abhandlungen*, vol. 1 (Leipzig, 1914), pp. 18–20; vol. 2, pp. 47–50; and my *Meinong*, pp. 11–18.

like Twardowski, Meinong, and Husserl, one does not sharply distinguish between these two relationships, then it may happen that one confuses the complex that is the individual with the complex that is the property.

But if one does confuse these two distinct entities with each other, then one may also be led to hold that the golden mountain is golden and that the round square is both round as well as square. For, the complex property of being round and square consists of the property *round* as well as of the property *square*. And since to say of an individual thing that it has a certain property is to say that it consists (in part) of this property, one may conclude that the round square must be round as well as square.

If one thinks of an individual thing, not as a complex of properties or instances, but as a separate entity which stands in a certain relationship – the exemplification nexus – to its properties, then one is less likely to confuse it with the corresponding complex property. While this property may be said to *consist* of its constituent properties, the individual does not then consist, in any sense of the word, of its properties. Rather, it *has* these properties; it exemplifies them. But even the traditional view, according to which individual things are substances rather than collections of properties, is not entirely immune against the confusion under discussion. For this view sometimes involves the identification of a substance with its nature, and a nature may be viewed as akin to a complex property.[24] Thus if we believe that substances have natures, we must also sharply distinguish between a substance and its nature. While a substance *has* certain properties, these properties are *parts of* its nature. And if we sharply distinguish between an individual thing (a substance), on the one hand, and the corresponding complex property (its nature), on the other, then we will be less tempted to claim that the golden mountain is golden and that the round square is both round and square. The golden mountain cannot *be* golden, since there is no such individual to begin with. But, of course, this is not to deny that the property of being golden and a mountain *consists* of the property of being golden and of the property of being a mountain.

That Twardowski indeed confuses individual things with the corresponding complex properties can be seen from his discussion of characteristics (*Merkmale*). Recall in this connection Frege's distinction between characteristics and properties (*Eigenschaften*).[25] According to

[24] I think that a confusion between substance and nature may be involved in Descartes' discussion of the properties of a nonexistent triangle in the fifth meditation.

[25] See Frege's "On Concept and Object," in *Translations from the Philosophical Writings of Gottlob Frege.*

Frege, the characteristics of a property are the properties of which it consists. Thus the characteristics of a property are, not characteristics of an individual thing which has this property, but are properties of that individual. For example, assume that $F$ is a complex property consisting of the two properties $G$ and $H$, and that $A$ is an individual which has $F$. $F$ is then a property of $A$, and so, of course, are $G$ and $H$. But $G$ and $H$ are not properties of $F$; they are characteristics of $F$. And they are not characteristics of $A$, since they are properties of $A$. Now, compare Frege's account with Twardowski's. Twardowski protests, justifiedly I think, against the common confusion between an idea and its parts, on the one hand, and the corresponding intention and its parts (the object and its parts), on the other. But he does not seem to notice that this confusion has two sides to it. Firstly, there is the traditional idealistic confusion between an idea and what it is an idea of; this is the confusion which Twardowski justifiedly criticizes. But, secondly, there is also a confusion between a complex property and the individual which has the properties that occur in this complex property; for, the complex idea is often identified – in the idealistic fashion – not with a complex property, its intention, but with an individual thing. While Twardowski avoids the first confusion, he does not avoid the second. As a result, he says that the constituent properties of $F$ are characteristics, not of $F$, but of the individual $A$.

One possible reason, then, for attributing properties to nonexistent objects seems to consist in a confusion between the nexus of exemplification and the part-whole relation. To see another possible reason, we shall take a look at Russell's objections to Meinong's position.[26]

Russell presents two arguments against Meinong's version of the second main thesis. Firstly, Russell points out that Meinong's claim about the properties of the round square implies that the law of contradiction does not hold for such entities. Meinong replies to this argument, and I think correctly, that this law was never supposed to hold for nonexistent objects in general and impossible objects in particular. Russell objects, secondly, that if the round square is really round, then the existing round square must really exist and, hence, we could easily prove the existence of a round square. Meinong's reply to this second objection is somewhat involved and not altogether clear.[27] He distinguishes between existing and existence. The existing round square,

[26] See Russell's review of the *Untersuchungen zur Gegenstandstheorie und Psychologie*.
[27] See Meinong's *Ueber Moeglichkeit und Wahrscheinlichkeit* (Leipzig, 1915), pp. 276–289.

he says, is indeed existing, but it does not exist. I think that this curious reply may be explicated in the following way. (1) Just as one can conceive of something which is both round and square, so one can conceive of something as existing. (2) What one does when one conceives of something as existing is to ascribe to it a certain property called "existing," but one does not thereby ascribe to it existence. (3) If one conceives of something as existing, than it does indeed have this property of existing, just as it may have both the property of being round as well as the property of being square. (4) But from the fact that something has the property of existing it does not follow that it exists. (5) Finally, and most importantly, one can never conceive of something having existence, unless it exists.

Since Meinong concedes in (1) that one can just as much think of something as existing as think of it as having such "ordinary" properties as being round and being square, he cannot answer Russell's objection by saying that existence is not a property and, hence, does not behave like one when it comes to what one can think of. As (2) shows, to the contrary, existence – in the form of existing – is turned into an "ordinary" property, that is, into a property for which the implicit principle holds that, if the property is conceived of as belonging to something, then it belongs to it. It is this principle that leads to Meinong's difficulty. That this difficulty is not avoided by Meinong's distinction appears quite clearly when we evaluate (5). Here Meinong maintains, in effect, that whenever we mistakenly believe that something exists, we do not really believe that it exists, but merely believe that it is existing.[28]

Be that as it may, however, I wish to call attention to the implicit principle just mentioned. According to this principle, such nonexistent objects as the golden mountain and the round square have precisely those properties which they are conceived of as having (which they are imagined to have, which they are believed to have, etc.). In answer to the question what properties Pegasus has, for example, we have to find out what properties Pegasus is (commonly) imagined to have. And this suggests very strongly that the second main thesis of the theory of entities and of phenomenology concerning the properties of nonexistent intentions may also arise from a confusion between what properties

[28] Meinong faces the same difficulty in connection with the factuality of objectives. Since one can mistakenly believe that a certain state of affairs is factual, Meinong must here, too, distinguish between full factuality (comparable to existence) and "watered down" factuality (comparable to existing), and he must claim that one cannot believe that a state of affairs has full factuality if it does not.

things have and what properties they are imagined to have. Avoiding this confusion, we shall insist, in the spirit of Russell's objection, that the golden mountain is not golden, but merely imagined to be golden, and that the round square is neither round nor square, but merely conceived of as being round and square. While it is true that when we think of the round square, we are thinking of something *as being* round and square, it is not true that we are thinking of something that *is* round and square.

## 4. THE INCOMPLETENESS OF OBJECTS

In chapter 13, Twardowski maintains that the constituents of every object which is presented by an idea divide into two groups: there are constituents of the object which are presented by partial ideas, but there are also many constituents of the object which are not presented by corresponding parts of its idea. In short, not all of the parts of an object are presented by the corresponding idea. Twardowski then goes on to call the parts of an object which are presented by its idea *characteristics* of the object.

Twardowski's view leads to a problem almost immediately. Recall Moore's famous example of the inkstand of which, so Moore claims, he can never see the whole.[29] Putting the matter in Twardowski's terms, this inkstand has a very large number of material and formal parts, that is, it has numerous properties and stands in all kinds of relations to other things. However, there is no idea which is so complex that it contains partial ideas of all of these properties and relations. No single idea thus intends the "whole" inkstand with all of its properties and all of its relations. But if this is true, and this is the problem, what right do we have to speak, as Twardowski does, of a particular idea as the idea of the inkstand? There is then obviously no such thing. Nor do we really have ideas of all the other perceptual objects we are constantly talking about. In Twardowski's own words: "There is no *adequate* idea of any object."

We must therefore carefully distinguish between the *intention* of an idea and the *object* of the idea. The intention of an idea comprises just those properties, features, aspects, or parts of an object which are presented by means of the idea and its parts. If we use the term 'characteristic' in Twardowski's sense, then we can say that the intention of an idea consists solely of the characteristics of the object. The object

[29] See Moore's "Some Judgments of Perception," in *Philosophical Studies* (London, 1922).

of the idea, on the other hand, is an "infinitely" complex bundle of properties and relations. This bundle is so complex that it can never be the intention of a single idea. What our ideas intend, therefore, are never the "real" perceptual objects, but, at best, certain properties, features, aspects, or parts of them. And this, if true, raises the question of how we know, not certain properties, features, aspects, or parts, but "whole" perceptual objects. Twardowski, we may surmise, is not fully aware of this problem because of an ambiguity in the word 'object.' The object of an idea, in one sense of the word, is simply the intention of the idea. In another sense of the word, though, the object of an idea is an individual thing, for example, an inkstand. When Twardowski claims that only certain parts of the perceptual object are objects of the corresponding idea, he uses 'objects' in the first sense. When he says that the (perceptual) object of the idea is infinitely complex, he uses 'object' in the second sense.

Both Meinong and Husserl reach the same conclusion as Twardowski, and essentially along the same line: There are no adequate ideas of objects. Both Meinong and Husserl, therefore, must also distinguish between the intentions of ideas and their objects. Meinong calls these intentions "incomplete objects," while Husserl speaks of "noemata."[30] And both of these philosophers hold that objects can only be given to a mind *through* the intentions of our ideas; they themselves can never be intentions. Thus they face the same problem as Twardowski: If the mind is never directly presented with an object, how do we know that there are any objects? And even if we can know that there are objects, how could we possibly know that two intentions belong to the same object? Twardowski and his followers thus are faced with the traditional but infamous dialectic surrounding the epistemological distinction between a phenomenal and a noumenal world. This dialectic has many versions. The Cartesian version concerns ideas and their intentions: Since what we really know are merely our own ideas, how can we possibly know anything about their intentions? The Kantian version concerns phenomena and things in themselves: Since what we really are presented with are phenomena as they appear to minds, how can we possibly know what things are like when they do not appear to a mind? Twardowski's version, it is clear, differs from both of these earlier ones. It arises from the obvious fact that single acts of perception

[30] See Meinong's *Ueber Moeglichkeit und Wahrscheinlichkeit* and Husserl's *Ideas. General Introduction to Pure Phenomenology* (London, 1971), For a most recent version of this view see Hector-Neri Castañeda, "Thinking and The Structure of the World," *Philosophia* 4 (1974).

never present us with all the properties, features, aspects, or parts of a perceptual object.

I do not think that there is a satisfactory solution to Twardowski's problem. If no idea is adequate, then it is hard to see how we could have any notion whatsoever of a "complete" object. What would the idea of a "complete" object be like? It could not be the idea of a round, green, heavy, etc. object; for, no matter how many properties we try to think through the idea, these properties will not exhaust all of the properties (and relations) of the complete object. Meinong is well aware of this problem. He tries to get around it by adding the property of completeness to the properties which we have to think of in order to think of a complete object.[31] But even he has some doubts about the effectiveness of this way out.

Furthermore, even if we can have a notion of a complete object, how could we ever know that two (or more) intentions belong to the same object? I believe that there is only one way in which we can decide this; we must, on some occasions, be acquainted, not only with certain parts of an object, but with the (whole) object itself. Only if we are acquainted with the (whole) object, can we find out that another intention is a part of it; and only if we are acquainted with the (whole) object, can we find out that two other intentions are parts of this same object. All other answers to the question simply introduce further mysteries. Neither Kant's postulation of the transcendental unity of apperception nor Husserl's elaborate theory in terms of memory and expectation will do.

If this diagnosis ic correct, then we are at once led to take a closer look at the source of these difficulties, at the proposition that there are no adequate ideas. Why do Twardoswki, Meinong, and Husserl all believe that it is impossible to perceive a complete object in one act of perception? I think that their assay of objects as collections of properties – in the style of Berkeley – may be the reason. If an inkstand is (identical with) an infinite bundle of properties (or of instances of properties), then it may appear obvious, since we never perceive infinitely many properties in one act of perception, that we cannot perceive the whole inkstand. On the other hand, if we conceive of the inkstand, not as a collection of properties, but as an individual thing – in the spirit of Descartes – which exemplifies numerous properties, but does not consist of them, then there is no reason to believe that we cannot perceive this individual thing (and some of its properties) in one

[31] *Ueber Moeglichkeit und Wahrscheinlichkeit*, p. 189.

act of perception. According to this alternative analysis, it is one thing to perceive the individual with some of its properties, quite another thing to perceive the sum total of all of its numerous properties; and while the latter may be impossible, the former is not.

But even if we take Twardowski's, Meinong's, and Husserl's side and think of the inkstand as a bundle of properties, it does not really follow that the inkstand as a whole cannot be perceived in one act of perception. Assume that the perceptual object $P$ consists of the properties $F$, $G$, $H$, etc., such that it is true that $P$ is identical with the collection consisting of $F$, $G$, $H$, etc. Assume further that we never perceive all of the properties $F$, $G$, $H$, etc. in one act of perception. Now, in order to get the conclusion that we can never perceive the perceptual object $P$ in one act of perception, another premise is required. This premise states that to perceive $P$ in one act of perception is to perceive all of the properties $F$, $G$, $H$, etc. (as connected with each other in a certain way, of course). But this premise is, in my opinion, false. To perceive $P$ is not to perceive all of the properties $F$, $G$, $H$, etc., even though $P$ consists of $F$, $G$, $H$, etc. In general: To perceive a whole is not, *ipso facto*, to perceive all of its parts. Perception, we must recall, is "intentional." From the fact that the inkstand before me is identical with the inkstand that has a nick on one of its sides it does not follow that when I see the inkstand before me, I am seeing an inkstand with a nick on one of its sides. As I would prefer to put the matter, the fact that *this thing* ($P$) exists is not the same as the fact that *the thing* ($P$) *which consists of* $F$, $G$, $H$, *etc.* exists, so that one may perceive the one without perceiving the other.

If these considerations are sound, then we are not forced to hold that complete objects cannot be perceived in single acts of perception. Nor do we have to conclude that, if they can be perceived at all, they must be perceived "through" incomplete objects. Instead we can revert to the commonsense view that we sometimes perceive a (complete) object without, at the same time, perceiving all of its properties.

## 5. INCOMPLETE OBJECTS AND DEFINITE DESCRIPTIONS

Every name, according to Twardowski, has both a meaning and a designation. Its meaning is an idea, a mental entity; its designation is the intention of this idea, the object of which the idea is an idea. Twardowski extends this distinction also to definite descriptions. The definite description expression 'the birthplace of Mozart,' for example, expresses an idea and designates an object. Twardowski claims, furthermore, that two descriptions of the same object express different ideas, but designate the same entity. For example, the designation of 'the city at the site of the Roman Juvavum' is the same at that of 'the birthplace of Mozart.' But the ideas expressed by these two expressions are different. There is thus some similarity between Twardowski's and Frege's accounts of definite descriptions. Frege distinguishes between the sense and the reference of a description expression; Twardowski distinguishes between the meaning and the designation of such an expression. But there is also a great difference between their respective views. While Twardowski's designation may be identified with Frege's reference the same is not the case for Twardowski's meaning and Frege's sense. Meanings are mental entities – individual ideas or concepts in the mind – while Frege's senses are nonmental. Frege, of course, does not deny that there are such mental things as ideas, but these things are not the senses of description expressions.

Since we can distinguish between different descriptions of the same entity it is quite obvious that we must distinguish between a description – roughly, Frege's sense and Twardowski's meaning – and the entity described – succinctly, Frege's reference and Twardowski's designation.[32] But while it is quite clear in a particular case what kind of entity is described, it is not equally clear what kind of entity a description is. The most important ontological question of any theory of descriptions is precisely this: To what category of entity do descriptions belong?[33] Frege, we all know, says that descriptions are nonmental objects (senses, in his terminology). Twardowski, we just saw, thinks that they are mental objects (ideas). I believe that Frege is more nearly correct than Twardowski.

Twardowski, it seems to me, is wrong when he identifies the intentions of the two description expressions mentioned earlier. The expression 'the city at the site of the Roman Juvavum' does not just express a different idea from the expression 'the birthplace of Mozart,' it also represents a different intention. But, of course, this is not to say that the two expressions describe different entities; they do describe

[32] By a "description" I do not here mean a linguistic exression, but whatever it is that can be translated from one language into another, so that we may say that the same description of a certain entity was given in English and in German.

[33] For a detailed discussion of this question and an answer see my "Definite Descriptions," *Philosophical Studies*, 27 (1975), 127–144; and my forthcoming "Structures, Functions, and Forms" in a collection of essays on Frege edited by M. Schirn and published in Germany by Frommann.

the very same city. If we heed our previous distinction between an intention and an object, then we can say that the two expressions represent different intentions, but describe the same object. Since Twardowski does not make this distinction, he can believe that the two ideas involved stand in the intentional nexus to the same entity, a certain city. But Twardowski comes very close to recognizing his mistake. He says that one conceives of something quite different when one conceives once of the city located at the site of the Roman Juvavum, once of the birthplace of Mozart. What one conceives of by means of an idea is quite obviously the intention of the idea. Thus it follows from this remark that the intentions of the respective ideas must be different. And this means that in one sense of the term 'object,' their objects must be different. Nor could this be otherwise; for Twardowski himself claims that the first idea contains as a part the idea of Rome, while the second does not contain this idea, but contains the idea of a certain composer. If so, how could the first idea fail to set Rome before the mind, and how could the second idea fail to present Mozart to the mind? And if these ideas present the mind with such different partial intentions, how could their complete intentions possibly be the same?

Twardowski does not draw this conclusion, even though it is implied in what he says. Instead, he convinces himself that the two ideas must have the same intention, since the city located at the site of the Roman Juvavum has all the properties of Mozart's birthplace. But from this application of Leibniz's principle it follows merely that the described entities are the same, not that the intentions of the two ideas are the same. We must therefore distinguish, not only between the idea expressed by a description expression and the entity which is described by means of the expression, but also between these two entities and the intention of the idea in question. This intention is the description mentioned earlier. Thus Frege's theory is more nearly correct than Twardowski's; for Frege does distinguish between the idea on the one hand and two further entities on the other, namely, the sense and the reference of the description expression. Furthermore, it is not entirely absurd to interpret Frege's senses (of description expressions) as the intentions of corresponding ideas.[34]

Meinong and Husserl at first accept Twardowski's theory of the meaning of descriptions. They, too, identify descriptions with ideas rather

[34] Compare, for example, Frege's illustration of the relationship between idea, sense, and reference in terms of an observation of the moon through a telescope, in "On Sense and Reference."

than with intentions of ideas. However, both of these philosophers later on develop theories in which they distinguish between ideas and descriptions; theories, therefore, which are more like Frege's. This very distinction, though, raises once more what I called earlier the most important ontological question of any theory of descriptions, namely, the question to what ontological category descriptions belong.

Recall now that Meinong and Husserl had already arrived, independently of any consideration of descriptions, at a distinction between intentions and objects in the form of the distinction between incomplete and complete objects. Nothing may seem therefore more natural, at least on first glance, than to identify incomplete objects with descriptions and complete objects with the entities described by descriptions. Indeed, there are some recent articles in which it is claimed that Husserl's noemata (incomplete objects, in Meinong's terminology) are really Fregean senses.[35] But even though Husserl – and Meinong as well – talks at times as if noemata are what Frege calls senses, an identification of these two kinds of entity is not at all plausible. The relation between an incomplete object and "its" complete object is that of part to whole; the incomplete object is a constituent of the complete object.[36] The relation between a description and what it describes, on the other hand, is quite obviously not of this sort.[37] To whatever category the entity *the birthplace of Mozart* may belong, this entity is most certainly not a part of Salzburg.

But what happens if we think of incomplete objects, not as complexes of properties, but as complex properties, and if we, furthermore, conceive of the relation between such an incomplete object and its corresponding complete object, not as that of part to whole, but rather as that of a property to the entity which has the property? Could one not identify noemata so conceived with Fregean senses? I do not think so. If Frege's view is clear on one point, it is the point that the relationship between the sense of a description expression and the corresponding reference is not that of a property (Frege says: "concept") to a subsumed object. How could it be, since senses are objects rather than properties (concepts) in Frege's ontology? That incomplete objects

[35] See, for example, Hubert L. Dreyfus, "*Sinn* and Intentional Object," in *Phenomenology and Existentialism*, Robert C. Solomon ed. (New York, 1972); and Dagfinn Føllesdal, "Husserl's Notion of Noema," *ibid.*

[36] Meinong speaks later in this connection of a relation of being "implektiert": the incomplete object is "implektiert" in the complete object. See his *Ueber Moeglichkeit and Wahrscheinlichkeit*, pp. 209–212.

[37] For a discussion and explication of this relationship see my forthcoming "Structures, Functions, and Forms."

(noemata) are not Fregean senses can only surprise those who do not realize that the philosophical dialectic which leads to the introduction of incomplete objects (noemata) is entirely different from the dialectic that leads to the introduction of descriptions. The former revolves around the alleged fact that no idea is adequate, that no complete individual thing can be presented to us in one act of perception, while the latter revolves around the undeniable fact that one can and must distinguish between descriptions and the entities they describe.

But aside from the question of whether or not incomplete objects, conceived of as complex properties, are Frege's senses, there is the interesting question of whether or not an identification of incomplete objects with complex properties, together with an identification of complete objects with the entities which have these properties, has any philosophical merit. It has been argued that the later Husserl made this twofold identification and that his view, as a consequence, avoids some of the difficulties inherent in Meinong's pronouncements about the golden mountain.[38] I do not think that this view, whether it is in the spirit of Husserl or not, has any advantages over Meinong's.

Firstly, the dialectic of the problem of nonexistent objects is not advanced by this identification. Compare the golden mountain with an existing brown mountain. The intention of the idea of the former is presumably a complex property; and so is the intention of the idea of the latter. In either case, the intention is a complex property rather than an individual thing. But by having a certain property as one's intention of the idea, it is claimed, one has a certain individual thing before the mind, namely, the individual which has the property. To have a certain individual before the mind and to have an idea with a certain complex property as intention is one and the same thing. Furthermore, an individual thing can be before the mind in this fashion even if it has no being. If this were not true, then one could simply not think at all of the golden mountain. But how can the golden mountain *have* the properties of being golden and of being a mountain, we may ask, if there is no such thing as the golden mountain? According to the view under discussion, the golden mountain – as distinguished from the complex property of being golden and a mountain – can only be brought before the mind if it stands in the nexus of exemplification to the corresponding complex property. This nexus thus takes the place

[38] See Guido Kung, "The World as Noema and as Referent," *Journal of the British Society for Phenomenology*, 3 (1972), 15–26; and, by the same author, "Noema und Gegenstand," in *Jenseits von Sein and Nichtsein*, R. Haller ed. (Graz, 1972).

of the intentional nexus in the argument between Twardowski and Russell. If one holds that this nexus can obtain between a property and an entity which lacks being, then one adopts in essence Twardowski's position, according to which there are relations of this sort. If one holds that it cannot obtain between a property and an entity which lacks being, then one is forced to conclude, as the early Russell does, that the golden mountain must have some sort of being after all.

Secondly, if the relation between the intention of an idea and its ultimate object is that of exemplification, then it follows immediately that the golden mountain is golden. Thus the identification of incomplete objects (noemata) with complex properties and of complete objects with the individuals which have these complex properties leads directly to Twardowski's and Meinong's view that nonexistent objects have properties. It does not, as has been claimed, avoid this view.

Thirdly, this identification runs into a difficulty of its very own. If to intend a complex property (by means of an idea whose intention it is) is the same as to have before the mind an individual which has this property, what then would it be like to have before the mind, not an individual, but a property? For example, what would it be like to think, not of the golden mountain, but of the property of being golden and a mountain? Is there another property in this case which stands to the property of being golden and a mountain in the same relationship in which the latter stands to the golden mountain? And if so, what is this property? I cannot think of any plausible answer. And this convinces me that the relationship between a mind and what is before it cannot be the complex relationship which consists (a) of the relation between an idea and its intended complex property and (b) of the relation between this complex property and an individual which has it. Rather, this relationship is the intentional nexus; and this nexus holds, not only between ideas and properties, but also between ideas and individual things.

To sum up, I have tried to indicate in this introduction that some of the most fundamental postulates of Meinong's theory of entities and of Husserl's phenomenology are anticipated in Twardowski's work. In particular, Twardowski held that the idea of the round square has an intention just as much as the idea of an existing round object; and he also held that the round square has certain properties, even though it has no being. But Twardowski's little book does not only contain the foundations of Meinong's and Husserl's later views, it also harbors the ingredients for some difficult problems which beset those later views.

In particular, Twardowski's argument that no idea is adequate leads eventually to all the strained attempts of Meinong's and Husserl's to explain how we are acquainted with ordinary perceptual objects, even though we are never presented with anything but small parts of them.

# 1. ACT, CONTENT, AND OBJECT OF THE PRESENTATION

It is one of the best known positions of psychology, hardly contested by anyone, that every mental phenomenon intends an immanent object. The existence of such a relation is a characteristic feature of mental phenomena which are by means of it distinguished from the physical phenomena. There always corresponds to the mental phenomena of being presented with something, of judging, of desiring, and of detesting something presented, something judged, something desired, and something detested, and the former would be an absurdity without the latter. This fact – mentioned by the Scholastics and even earlier by Aristotle – has recently been appreciated in its great importance by Brentano who, among other things, has based the classification of mental phenomena on the kinds of relations which obtain between the presentation and what is presented, etc.[1]

On the basis of this relation to an "immanent object," which is characteristic of mental phenomena, one has become accustomed to distinguish for every mental phenomenon between act and content, and thus each of them appears from two sides. When one talks about "presentations," one can understand by this expression sometimes the act of presenting; sometimes, however, one can mean by it what is presented, the content of the presentation. And hence it has become customary to use instead of the expression 'presentation' one of the two expressions 'act of presenting' and 'content of presentation' whenever the smallest possibility of a misunderstanding exists.

But if a confusion between the mental act and its content is thus prevented, an ambiguity – pointed out by Hoefler – still remains to be overcome. After having discussed the characteristic relation of mental phenomena to a content, he continues: "(1). What we called "content of the presentation and the judgment" lies just as much completely

[1] Franz Brentano, *Psychologie vom empirischen Standpunkt* (Leipzig, 1874), vol. 2, chapter 1, para. 5; and chapter 6, para. 2.

within the subject as the act of presentation and of judgment itself. (2) The words 'thing' and 'object' are used in two senses: on the one hand for that *independently existing* entity ... at which our presentation and judgment aim, as it were; on the other hand, for the mental, more or less approximate, "picture" of that real entity which *exists "in" us*. This quasi-picture (more accurate: sign) is identical with the content mentioned under (1). In distinction to the thing or object, which is assumed to be independent of thinking, one also calls the content of a presentation and judgment (similarly: of a feeling and willing) the "*immanent or intentional* object" of these mental phenomena."[2]

One has to distinguish, accordingly, between the object at which our idea "aims, as it were," and the immanent object or the content of the presentation. This distinction is not always made and has been overlooked by, among others, Sigwart.[3] Language facilitates here, too, as so often, our mistaking one thing for another in that it lets the content as well as the object be "presented." It will also turn out that the expression 'the presented' is in a similar fashion ambiguous as is the expression 'presentation.' The latter serves just as much to designate the act and the content as the former serves to designate the content, the immanent object, and also the non-immanent object, the object of the presentation.

The present investigation is concerned with a detailed separation of the presented, in one sense, where it means the content, from the presented in the other sense, where it is used to designate the object – in short, of the content of the presentation from the object of the presentation – and with the mutual relationship between the two.

[2] *Logic*. Written, in collaboration with Dr. Alexius Meinong, by Dr. Alois Hoefler (Wien, 1890), para. 6.

[3] Compare Hillebrand, *Die neuen Theorien der kategorischen Schluesse* (Wien, 1891), para. 23.

# 2. ACT, CONTENT, AND OBJECT OF THE JUDGMENT

It appears likely that judgments are similar to presentations in regard to the distinction between content and object. If it is possible to discover a difference also between the content and the object of the mental phenomenon called judgment, then this should help to clarify the analogous relationship for presentations.

What distinguishes presentations from judgment and makes them into sharply separated classes of mental phenomena is the special kind of intentional relationship to an object. In what this relationship consists, cannot be described; it can only be elucidated by reference to inner experience. And here the difference between the ways in which a mental act can relate to an object emerges very clearly. For, quite obviously, it is in each case a different relation whether someone is merely presented with something or whether he affirms it or denies it. There are no transitional stages between these two kinds of intentional relation, neither continuous ones nor discontinuous ones. It is a crass misapprehension of the facts if one believes that in the middle between presentations and judgments there exist certain transitional forms; B. Erdmann postulates such forms of transition. "When we remember," he says, "an object, when we form an abstract idea, or when we try to get clear about the characteristics of a complex object, then we relate the successively appearing characteristics to the object automatically and, almost without exception, with the help of presentations of words. And this in such a way that they are attributed to the object, predicated of it, so that the latter is conceived of as the subject, and the former, as the predicates, of a judgment. Presentations thus blend into judgments; they occur in a predicative presentational process." And further: "From the opposite direction, too, the distinction between presentation and judgment is a gradual one ... For we can also sum up judgments in one word. Words like 'categorical imperative,' 'state,' 'justice,' 'police,' 'religion,' 'value' (in the economic sense), 'goods,' 'law of nature,' have their meaning, not in presentations, but in judgments which, like presentations, are summed up in a word, but which nevertheless appear in consciousness only as judgments. Whenever their meaning is clear, it is given in judgments, in definitions; and the process of abstraction, through which they come about, is mediated by language."[1] These are Erdmann's arguments for the existence of a transition from presentations to judgments, and conversely; a transition which has also been asserted by others.[2] It is easy to show the mistake in Erdmann's explanations.

Concerning Erdmann's first argument, according to which we always involuntarily relate the characteristics of a complex object to the object in such a way that the latter is conceived of as the subject, the former, as predicates of a judgment, this argument is not sound. For, even if it would have to be admitted that being presented with a complex object happens in just the way described by Erdmann, the occurrence of judgments or of a transition form between presentations and judgments would not have been demonstrated. If one thinks of an object as the subject and of its characteristics as predicates of a judgment, then one conceives of a judgment-subject, of judgment-predicates, and of the judgments themselves, since subject and predicate as such can only be conceived of in conjunction with a simultaneous reflection upon a judgment. However, there is obviously a great difference between the conception of a judgment and the making of a judgment. A conceived judgment as little constitutes a judgment as a merely conceived "hundred coins" constitute an ownership. Therefore, even if a complex object can be presented only with the help of "predicative presentation processes," the attributing of certain characteristics to an object as a subject is nevertheless only a presented attributing and as different from a real attributing, from a judgment, as the painted fairy castle is from a real one. If one is presented with the complex object *gold*, then one is presented with gold as being yellow, as glittering metallically, as being heavy, etc. This means that the judgments "Gold is yellow," "Gold glitters metallically," "Gold is heavy," etc. are all presented; but these judgments are merely presented, not made. If they were

[1] B. Erdmann, *Logik* (Halle a.S., 1892), vol. 1, para. 34.

[2] Compare Bosanquet, *Logic* (Oxford, 1888), vol. 1, p. 41: "An idea or concept is not an image, though it may make use of images. It is a habit of judging with reference to a certain identity. ... The purpose ... was to show, that the acts set in motion by the name and by the proposition are the same, and therefore the logical function of the forms would not be generically different." Similarly, Schmitz-Dumont: "State rights means the same as when we say, more explicitly, the state has certain rights." *Vierteljahrsschrift fuer wissenschaftliche Philosophy*, vol. 10 (1886), p. 205.

made, as Erdmann maintains, then one could never be *presented* with a complex object, an object analyzed in regard to its characteristics, without *asserting* something true or false about the object. This consequence, if pursued in all directions, would yield the corollary that there are only *simply* presentations in the true sense of the word; and with this Erdmann himself would not agree.

Erdmann's second argument for the existence of transitional stages between the class of presentations and that of judgments is, on closer view, merely the converse of the first and just as unsound. It is to be admitted, certainly, that judgments can be summed up in a word. And this is possible in two ways. A judgment which finds its usual linguistic expression in a sentence can either be expressed by a sentence which consists of only a single word, or it can be pronounced without the occurrence of a sentence. The first is the case in many languages for so-called subjectless sentences; for example, in Greek, Latin, and all Slavic languages. In this case, the judgment is summed up by means of a word, because the sentence that means the judgment appears to be represented by a single word. But the judgment can also be summed up in a word when the latter does not represent a sentence in the grammatical sense. Whoever screams "Fire!" or the like condenses the sentence 'It is burning' and the judgment meant by this sentence into a single word.

Different from these cases is the one which Erdmann has in mind. It is true that, whenever the meaning of words like 'state,' 'justice,' etc. is clear, it is given by means of definitions. Now, definitions are undoubtedly sentences. But Erdmann has overlooked the point that to sentences there can correspond as a mental correlate not only judgments, but also many other things; for example, wishes and the like. In addition to genuine judgments, merely presented judgments are also communicated by means of sentences. When someone describes the object of his presentation, then he uses for this purpose sentences. He says: "The piece of gold with which I am presented is yellow," etc. But in this way no other judgment is expressed than that the speaker has a certain presentation; no judgment is made about the object of the presentation itself. Rather, judgments about the condition of the piece of gold are merely presented. And it is these presented judgments which are expressed in the definition which itself appears in the form of one or more sentences. If the definition, as Erdmann maintains, has no other task than to give the clear meaning of a word, then the only judgment which it contains is a judgment about the connection which holds for the speaker between a certain name and a certain meaning. If someone says: "The state is a public commonwealth which embraces a people, inhabiting a certain region, in the union of the rulers and the ruled," then he has not expressed a judgment about the state, but has merely asserted that he refers by means of the word 'state' to an object whose presentation is put together in the manner indicated. And the description of this presentation proceeds with the help of sentences which consist of subject and predicate, but whose mental correlates, far from being judgments, are presentations of judgments. One sees how Erdmann's second argument ties in with the first one and stands or falls with it.

We shall, therefore, have to hold that presentation and judgment are two sharply separated classes of mental phenomena without intermediate forms of transition.

As far as the object of a judgment is concerned, the very same object which in one case is merely presented, can in another case also be judged; it can be affirmed or denied. That the nature of judgment consists, as it were, in affirmation or denial has been expounded by Brentano.[3] What is affirmed or denied is the subject of the judgment. Now, this mental activity which is directed toward an object is bound up with the existence or nonexistence of the object in a peculiar way. For, the object is judged; but in being affirmed, its existence appears also to be affirmed. If the object is denied, its existence appears also to be denied. But if someone now believes that the affirmation or denial of an object consists in the affirmation or denial of a connection between the characteristic "existence" and the object, then he fails to see that by means of the affirmation of a connection, the connected parts themselves are implicitly affirmed, while by means of a denial of a connection the parts are not denied. By means of the assertion of the existence of *A*, *A* itself is thus already affirmed; but by means of the denial of the existence of *A*, *A* is also denied, and this could not be the case, if we were dealing here with a connection between *A* and the characteristic "existence."[4] And yet the existence of *A* is affirmed by means of the affirmation of *A*, and by means of the denial of the existence of *A*, *A* is also denied.

This circumstance indicates that function of the act of judging which is the analogue to the function of the act of presentation by means of which, in addition to the object, its content as well is "presented."

[3] *Op. cit.*, vol. 2, chapter 7, para. 4 ff.
[4] *Ibid.*, para. 5.

Just as in the presenting of an object, toward which this presenting is directed in the real sense, something else occurs, namely, the content of the presentation – which is also "presented," but in a different sense from the object – so is that which is affirmed or denied through a judgment, without being the object of the judging behavior, the content of the judgment. The content of a judgment is thus the existence of an object, with which every judgment is concerned; for, whoever makes a judgment, asserts something about the existence of an object. In affirming or denying the object, he also affirms or denies its existence. What is judged in the real sense is the object itself; and in being judged, there is judged also, but in another sense, its existence.

The analogy with the situation which obtains in the area of presentations is a perfect one. Here as there, one has a mental act; here the judging, there the presentation. The former, just like the latter, relates to an object which is presumed to be independent of thinking. When the object is presented and when it is judged, in both cases there occurs a third thing, besides the mental act and its object, which is, as it were, a sign of the object: its mental "picture" when it is presented and its existence when it is judged. One says of the mental "picture" of an object and of its existence that the former is presented, the latter is judged. The real object of the presentation and judgment, however, is neither the mental picture of the object nor its existence, but the object itself. But as little as the mental picture or the existence of an object is identical with the object itself, so little is the sense of the respective verbs the same when one says of the content and object of a presentation that they are "presented," of the content and object of a judgment that they are "judged."

## 3. NAMES AND PRESENTATIONS

Although there is no complete parallelism between speaking and thinking, there exists, nevertheless, an analogy between the mental phenomena and the linguistic expressions which designate them, an analogy which may serve to elucidate the peculiarities of the one area in terms of the peculiarities of the phenomena of the other area. In regard to the distinction under discussion between the content and the object of a presentation, a look at names as the linguistic sign of presentations will render this service.

Even a question which has been raised about names proves that one has to distinguish between three things in regard to presentations. Mill asks, when he treats names, whether it is more appropriate to view names as names of things or of our presentations of things.[1] By "things" he understands here what we call the "objects" of presentations; by "presentations," he can only mean the contents of presentations, not the acts of presentation. The answer which Mill, following Hobbes, gives to this question presupposes straightforwardly a difference between the content and the object of a presentation. The word 'sun,' Mill maintains, is the name of the sun and not the name of our presentation of the sun; yet he does not want to deny that the presentation alone, and not the thing, is recalled through the name or communicated to a listener. The task of a name is thus twofold: the name communicates to a listener the content of a presentation and, at the same time, it names an object. However, we said that we must discern, not just a twofold, but a threefold aspect of every presentation: the act, the content, and the object. And if a name really yields an accurate linguistic picture of the mental state of affairs which corresponds to it, then it must also show a correlate to the act of presentation. Indeed, there is such a correlate; and to the three aspects of a presentation –

[1] Mill, *System der induktiven und deduktiven Logik*, transl. by *Th. Gomperz* (Leipzig, 1884), vol. 1, chapter 2, para. 1.

the act, the content, and the object – there corresponds a threefold task which every name has to fulfill.

By a name, one has to understand here everything that the old logicians called a categorematic sign. Now, categorematic signs are linguistic means of designation which do not have a meaning solely within a context (like 'of the father,' 'about,' 'nevertheless,' and the like), and which do not by themselves completely express a judgment (assertion), or a feeling, or a decision of the will, and the like (requesting, asking, commanding, etc.), but which are merely expressions for presentations. Such names are 'the founder of ethics' and 'a son, who has insulted his father.'[2]

What, then, is the task of names? Obviously, it is to arouse in the listener a certain content of a presentation.[3] Someone who utters a name intends to awaken in the listener the same mental content which appears in himself; when someone says: "sun, moon, and stars," he wants those who listen to think, just as he does, of the sun, the moon, and the stars. But in wanting to arouse in the listener a certain mental content through the utterance of a name, the speaker reveals, at the same time, to the listener that he, the speaker, finds this content in himself and is thus presented with the same thing with which he wants the listener to be presented.[4] In this manner, a name already fulfills two tasks. Firstly, it makes known that the user of the name is presented with something; it signifies the existence of a mental act in the speaker. Secondly, it awakens in the listener a certain mental content. It is this content which is the "meaning" of a name.[5]

However, this does not as yet exhaust the functions of a name. It has a third function, namely, the function of designating objects. Names are names of things, says Mill, and for the justification of this

[2] Marty, "Ueber subjectlose Saetze etc.," *Vierteljahrsschrift fuer wissenschaftliche Philosophie*, vol. 8 (1884), p. 293.

[3] Brentano, *op. cit.*, vol. 2, chapter 6, para. 3. *Marty, op. cit.*, p. 300; and Mill at the last mentioned place.

[4] Tones and other objects whose presentations are used to awaken in another person certain further presentations which are connected with them, are for that person most of the time, though not always, a sign that the mentioned presentations exist also in the mind of the person who produces those tones and other objects. Bolzano, *Wissenschaftslehre* (Sulzbach, 1837), para. 285.

[5] Etymologically the meaning of a name is that which we are caused to think of when the name is used (Jevons, *Principles of Science*, p. 25). We designate in every case as the meaning of an expression that mental content which it is the real task, the goal, of the name to arouse in the listener (be it from nature, be it through habit), if the name has the ability to achieve this goal regularly. In being a sign of the act of presentation which occurs in the speaker, the name is a sign of a presentation which the listener is supposed to awaken in himself. Only in making that fact known does the name mean this presentation. (Marty, at the last mentioned place.)

assertion he appeals to the fact that we use names in order to communicate something about things. The third task which a name has to fulfill is this – the designation of objects. Accordingly, the three functions of a name are: firstly, to make known an act of presentation which occurs in the speaker; secondly, to arouse a mental content, the meaning of the name, in the person addressed; thirdly, to designate an object which is presented through the presentation meant by the name.

This reference to the three tasks which every name fulfills thus confirms perfectly the distinction between the content and the object of a presentation. A consideration of the linguistic expression for a presentation offers us, therefore, the means to distinguish what otherwise could easily be confused or considered to be one and same thing, because of a linguistic imperfection which allows us to refer to a content as well as an object as "something presented."

# 4. THE "PRESENTED"

The fact that the expression 'to be presented' is ambiguous in that both the content as well as the object of a presentation are said to be presented makes a precise distinction between content and object more difficult. We have said already that the content and the object of a presentation are not in the same sense "something presented." We shall now try to determine what the expression 'presented' means when it is applied to the object of a presentation and what sense it has when it is applied to the content of a presentation. This difference in meaning appears if we recall the relationship between attributive or determining adjectives on the one hand and modifying adjectives on the other.[1]

A determination is called attributive or determining if it completes, enlarges – be it in a positive or in a negative direction – the meaning of the expression to which it is attached. A determination is modifying if it completely changes the original meaning of the name to which it is attached. Thus in 'good man' the determination 'good' is a truly attributive one; if one says 'dead man,' one uses a modifying adjective, since a dead man is not a man. Likewise, by adding the adjective 'false' to a name, the original meaning of this name is replaced by another; for a false friend is no friend and a false diamond is no diamond. There is the possibility that the same word is used sometimes modifying, at other times in a truly attributive manner. A case in point is the just mentioned adjective 'false.' In the earlier examples, it is undoubtedly a modifying adjective; not so in contexts like 'a false judgment,' 'a false (not faithful) man.'

The same holds for the determination in 'something is "presented."' However, before we pursue the ambiguity of this expression, we want to look at a completely analoguous case, which – being taken from outer experience – has the advantage of being well-known and of making us more adroit at grasping the ambiguity of the word 'presented.'

[1] Compare Brentano, *op. cit.*, vol. 2, chapter 7, para. 7 in the footnote on p. 288.

As is well known, one says that the painter paints a picture, but also that he paints a landscape. One and the same activity of the painter is directed toward two objects; the result of the activity is only one. After the painter has finished the painting of the picture and of the landscape, repectively, he has before him a painted picture as well as a painted landscape. The picture is painted; it is neither engraved, nor etched, etc.; it is a painted, real picture. The landscape, too, is painted, but it is not a real landscape, only a "painted one." The painted picture and the painted landscape are in truth only one; for the picture depicts a landscape, hence it is a painted landscape; the painted landscape is a picture of the landscape.

The word 'painted' plays therefore two roles. If used for the picture, it appears as a determination. It determines more closely the nature of the picture, according to which it is a painting, not an engraving, etching, woodcut, etc. On the other hand, when one says of the landscape that it is painted, then the determination 'painted' is modifying, because the painted landscape is not a landscape but a piece of canvas which has been treated by the painter according to certain laws of color distribution and perspective. The painted landscape is no longer a landscape, but a picture.

But this painted landscape, the picture, portrays a real landscape. The landscape which is painted by the painter – be it from nature or by using his imagination – is depicted by the picture, hence painted by the painter. It does not cease to be a landscape just because it has been painted by the painter. When I point at a landscape and add: "I remember this landscape, there was a picture of it at the art exhibition, it has been painted by the painter *X*," then I talk – calling the landscape in this sense "painted" – about the real landscape which has been painted, not about the painted landscape as it adorns a wall at the art exhibition. The addition 'painted,' attached in this sense to the word 'landscape,' does not modify the meaning of the word 'landscape' in the slightest. It is a genuinely determining addition which indicates that the landscape stands in a certain relationship to a picture; a relationship which just as little prevents the landscape from being a landscape as a man stops being a man just because he stands in the relation of similarity to another man because of his features.

What we said about the word 'painted' as applied to picture and landscape holds *mutatis mutandis* for the determination 'presented' as it applies to the content and the object of a presentation. And since one is used to characterize one's being presented with something as a kind of mental picturing, this facilitates the comparison between the painted landscape and the presented object and makes it a more suitable comparison than it may otherwise have been, since we are here comparing an inner with an outer experience.

To the verb 'to present,' there correspond – in a similar fashion as to the verb 'to paint' – first of all two things: an object which is presented and a content which is presented. The content is the picture; the object, the landscape. The result of the activity of presenting which moves in two directions is again only one. The presented object, in the sense in which the painted landscape is a picture, is the content of the presentation. The content which is presented in a presentation is truly a content; when applied to the content, the addition 'presented' is as little modifying as the addition of 'painted' is in regard to the picture. The presented content is just as much a content as the painted picture is a picture. Just as a picture can only be painted or created through some other activity, a content of a presentation can only be presented; no other activity can here replace the presenting. The content of a presentation and the presented object are one and the same thing. The expression 'presented' is a modifying determination of the object; for the presented object is no longer an object, but is merely the content of a presentation. The painted landscape, too, as we pointed out, is no longer a landscape, but a picture.

But we saw that the painted landscape, the picture, depicts something which is not in this very same sense something painted. Similarly, the content of a presentation aims at something which is not a content of a presentation, but which is an object of this presentation, in analogy to the way in which the landscape is the "subject" of the picture which depicts it. And just as the landscape is copied in this picture, just as it is depicted by it and, hence, "painted" in a sense different from the earlier one, so is the object which corresponds to a presentation pictured mentally, as one says – that is, presented through the content of this presentation. When one says of the object that it is presented in this last sense, then the meaning of the word 'object' is not at all modified; "The object is presented" says then only that an object has entered into a certain relationship with a being capable of having presentations. But thereby it has not ceased to be an object.

Hence, if one speaks of a "presented object," one can mean two different things. That an object is presented can mean that an object stands – among many further relations to other objects – also in a certain relation to a cognizant being which forms one of the relations two terms. In this sense, the presented object is a genuine object just like the extended, lost, etc. object. In another sense, however, the presented object is the opposite of a genuine object; the presented object is then no longer an object, but a content of a presentation, and it is something entirely different from the genuine object. It is the presented object in the first sense which can be affirmed or denied through a judgment. In order to be judged, the object has to be first presented; what is not presented can as little be affirmed or denied as it can be loved or hated. Yet the affirmed or denied object, the desired or detested object, is a presented object only in the second of the two mentioned meanings. The presented object in the first mentioned sense of the word 'presented' is not what is affirmed or denied; one does not have *it* in mind when one says that an object exists or does not exist. The presented object in this sense is the content of the presentation, the "mental picture" of an object.

The just discussed ambiguity of the word 'presented' has not always been taken into account. Sigwart, for example, confuses the presented object in the sense of the object of a presentation with the presented object in the sense of the content of a presentation when he argues against the idiogenetic theory of judgment.[2]

Similarly, Drobisch does not pay attention to the difference between the presented object in the one and the presented object in the other sense. When he speaks of the task which names have to fulfill, he says: "Insofar as thinking considers only *that* which is presented in presentation, the *presented*, and disregards all subjective conditions of being presented, it forms concepts. – The linguistic designation of a concept is the name. It is true that one views the name as the designation of the thing [Sache], of the real object of the presentation (if it has one); but that which is presented through a concept is simply nothing else but the thing which has become known."[3] Obviously, Drobisch does not notice that he uses an ambiguous word when he talks about the "presented," and he uses it, in fact, once with one meaning, once with another. When he characterizes the concept as that which is presented in a presentation, he means by the presented the *content* of the presentation; but when he says that the presented is nothing else but the thing which has become known, then one must understand by the presented the object of the presentation, inasmuch as it is the object of a presentation which is directed toward it. If Drobisch had paid attention to

[2] Sigwart, *Logik* (Freiburg i. B., 1889), vol. 1, para. 12.7.
[3] Drobisch, *Neue Darstellung der Logik* (Leipzig, 1875), para. 8.

this difference, he would not have characterized the name as a linguistic designation of the concept, but would have noticed that a name, though it does *mean* the concept (thus in Drobisch's sense the content of the presentation), names, because of this very fact, the object, the thing.

Drobisch makes the same mistake when he explains the difference between "characteristics" and "constituents."[4] "This difference," we read there, "does not consist in the fact that the former are parts of the concept, while the latter, on the other hand, are parts of the thing, of the object itself. This thing, too, and its parts are only something presented; we do not here go beyond concepts either." Drobisch thus sees no real difference between the concept and the thing, since both are "something presented." But that something can be "something presented" in different senses, once as content, once as object, seems to have escaped his attention.

However, the difference between the content and the object of a presentation has also often been stressed. Bolzano used to emphasize this difference and clung steadfastly to it.[5] Zimmermann warns explicitly against confusing the content with the object.[6] And Kerry has recently demonstrated this difference for the presentations of numbers, and hence for presentations whose objects are not real.[7] Later, we shall have occasion to refer to these scholars and to rely on their results in connection with a number of pending questions; for now, we merely want to describe more accurately the relationship which obtains between the content and the object of a presentation, on the one hand, and the act of presentation, on the other, as well as the terminology which we shall adopt for this relationship.

In comparing the act of presenting with painting, the content with the picture, and the object with the subject matter which is put on canvas – for example, a landscape – we have also more or less approximated the relationship between the act on the one hand and the content and the object of the presentation on the other. For the painter, the picture is the means by which to depict the landscape; he wants to picture, paint, a real or merely imagined landscape, and he does so in painting a picture. He paints a landscape in making, painting, a picture

[4] *Ibid.*, para. 14.

[5] Bolzano, *op. cit.*, para. 49. Instead of the expression "content of a presentation," Bolzano uses the term 'objective presentation,' 'presentation as such,' and he distinguishes from it the object on the one hand, on the other the 'experienced' or 'subjective' presentation by which he means the mental act of presentation.

[6] Zimmermann, *Philosophische Propaedeutik* (Wien, 1897), para. 18 and para. 26.

[7] Kerry, "Ueber Anschauung und ihre psychische Verarbeitung," *Vierteljahrsschrift* etc., vol. 10, and further.

of this landscape. The landscape is the "primary" object of his painting activity; the picture is the "secondary" object. Analogously for presentations. A person presents to himself some object, for example, a horse. In doing so, however, he presents to himself a mental content. The content is the copy of the horse in a sense similar to that in which the picture is the copy of the landscape. In presenting to himself an object, a person presents to himself at the same time a content which is related to this object. The presented object, that is, the object at which the presenting activity, the act of presentation, aims, is the primary object of the presenting. The content through which the object is presented is the secondary object of the presenting activity.[8]

In order to distinguish, then, between the two meanings attached to the word 'to present' when applied to the content and when applied to the object, we shall use Zimmermann's terminology.[9] We shall say of the content that it is thought, presented, *in* the presentation; we shall say of the object that it is presented *through* the content of the presentation (or through the presentation.) What is presented *in* a presentation is its content; what is presented *through* a presentation is its object. In this way it will be possible to retain the word 'to present' – to replace it by another word would only add to the confusion – and yet to avoid the misunderstandings which this word tends to cause because of its ambiguity. When one says that something is presented, one merely has to add whether it is presented *in* the presentation or *through* the presentation. In the first case, the presented means the content of the presentation; in the second, the object of the presentation.

We said that the content is the means, as it were, by which the object is presented. From this viewpoint, the analogy we found between the presentation and its linguistic expression, the name, appears again quite clearly. We have seen that it is the original function of the name to indicate a mental act, namely, an act of presentation. In this manner, the name arouses in the listener a meaning, a mental (presentation-) content; and the name designates an object in virtue of this meaning.[10]

[8] However, in Brentano the expressions 'primary object' and 'secondary object' occur in a somewhat different sense (*op. cit.*, vol. 2, chapter 2, para. 8). For, although Brentano calls the object of a presentation its primary object, just as we have, he understands by the secondary object of a presentation the act and content taken together, as far as they are both grasped through "inner consciousness" when the presentation of an object occurs and this presentation, therefore, becomes conscious.

[9] *Op. cit.*, at the mentioned places.

[10] G. Noël characterizes these two tasks of a content, namely, the task of being the meaning of the name and being that through which the object is presented, in the following way: D'une part l'idée est ce qui représente un objet à l'esprit; elle est en d'autres termes, le substitut mental de l'objet. D'autre part l'idée est ce qui constitute la signification d'un nom, l'acte, par

Hence, just as the name designates an object by means of the awakening of a content of a presentation, so the act of presentation (made known through the name) presents an object by means of the content itself.

Kerry tries to avoid the misunderstandings which occur if one speaks of a "presented" object without any further explanation by distinguishing between the "presented as such" and the "presented plain and simple.'[11] However, it is doubtful whether the intended result can be achieved in this fashion. For, when one attaches to a name an addition by means of a particle like 'as,' 'as far as,' etc., the listener is asked to present to himself the mentioned object from a certain definite point of view, through very definite characteristics, namely, those mentioned by the addition. This is the case, for example, when someone talks about the circle "as" the limiting case of the ellipse, or of the American monkey "as far as" all of them have tails. But if the expression added to the name by means of phrases like 'as' and 'as far as' is itself ambiguous, then the misunderstandings created by the name are not excluded. If one speaks, therefore, of an object as "presented," then one has not prevented the misunderstanding which can be created by the ambiguity in the word 'presented.' For, something can be viewed as "something presented" in two different senses, it may be the object or it may be the content of an act of presentation. In the first case, the addition 'as something presented' works really as a determination, since it calls attention to a relation between an object and a cognizant being. In the second case, the addition has a modifying effect; for a presented object in this sense is not an object, but is the content of a presentation.

We shall, therefore, adopt Zimmermann's terminology, which seems best suited to avoid all misunderstandings; and we shall say that the content is presented *in*, the object presented *through*, the presentation.

lequel nous conferons à ce nom un sens déterminé, une acception précise, exclusive de toute autre. ("Noms et Concepts," *Revue philosophique*, 31, p. 471). Compare also Marty, "Ueber das Verhaeltnis von Logik und Grammatik," in *Symbolae Pragensis*, Festgabe etc. (Wien, 1893), p. 116, footnote 1.

[11] Kerry, *op. cit.*, vol. 15, p. 135.

## 5. SO-CALLED "OBJECTLESS" PRESENTATIONS

Up to now, we have silently assumed that to every presentation without exception there corresponds an object. For every presentation, we have said, one must distinguish, not only the content from the act, but also from these entities a third one, namely, the object. Now, there is the obvious objection to this view that there are "objectless" presentations; presentations, to which there correspond no objects. If so, then our previous considerations would have to be greatly qualified; under no conditions could they hold for all presentations. Indeed, even those who have explicitly defended the distinction between the objects and the contents of presentations have believed that this distinction can only be maintained for one group of presentations; and they contrasted this group with another equally large or even larger group of presentations, namely, with presentations to which there correspond no objects and which, therefore, have to be called "objectless" presentations.

Bolzano thus teaches that there are objectless presentations, that is, presentations which have no object. According to Bolzano, if someone claims to find it absurd to maintain that a presentation has no object whatsoever and, hence, does not present something, then this can only be due to the fact that he confuses the content of a presentation – which indeed belongs to every presentation – with the object of the presentation. And as examples of such "objectless" presentations, Bolzano mentions the following: Nothing, round square, green virtue, golden mountain.[1] Kerry holds, similarly, that if one shows that the parts of a presentation are incompatible, then one has proven that this presentation cannot have an object. Such a presentation, for example, is the presentation of a number greater than zero which, when added to itself, equals itself.[2] Hoefler, too, teaches that

[1] Bolzano, *op. cit.*, para. 67.

[2] Kerry, *op. cit.*, vol. 10, 3. 428 and 444.

there are presentations "whose extensions are equal to zero, that is, to which there corresponds no object." As examples of such presentations, Hoefler lists, in addition to those mentioned by Bolzano, the presentations of a dirigible air-balloon, a diamond the size of a cubic foot, etc.[3]

Hence there are three kinds of presentation to which there correspond, presumably, no objects. Firstly, presentations which involve in a straightforward way the negation of any object, like the presentation *nothing*. Secondly, presentations to which there correspond no objects because their contents combine incompatible determinations, for example, *round square*. Thirdly, presentations to which there correspond no objects, because experience has up to now not presented us with one. We shall examine the arguments for the existence of such presentations with regard to these three kinds of "objectless" presentations.

1. In regard to the presentation designated by 'nothing,' there seems to exist a mistake which has occurred for hundreds of years in all logical and dialectical investigations. Quite a bit has been thought about the μὴ ὄν, the *non-ens* and *nihil*; it has been held that one must distinguish between different kinds of "nothing," and Kant still gives a survey of the four kinds of "nothing." Among these we find also the "nothing as empty concept without object."[4]

However, it is questionable whether the word 'nothing' is a categorematic expression, that is, whether this word designates a presentation at all, as such words as 'father,' 'judgment,' and 'foliage' do. The meaning of 'nihil' has in general been equated with that of 'non-ens,' and it is maintained these days also that 'nothing' simply substitutes for the expression 'not something.' If so, then it will be necessary to raise the question what expressions like 'non-ens' and 'not something' mean.

The combination of a categorematic expression with *non*, not – what the scholastics called infinitation – yields in general a new expression with a definite meaning. A presentation is dichotomically divided by an expression formed with "not."

But it is not the presentation whose name is preceded by the negative particle which is dichotomically divided. When one says 'non-Greek,' Greeks are not divided into those who are Greeks and those who are not. What is divided is a superordinate concept, for example,

[3] Hoefler, *op. cit.*, para. 6 and 17, 4.
[4] Kant, *Kritik der reinen Vernunft*, ed. Kehrbach, p. 259.

human beings. The situation is similar for infinitations like non-smoker, by means of which travelers are divided into those who smoke and those who do not. Only if one does not recognize this power of an infinitation to dichotomize a superordinate presentation can one arrive at the peculiar view that by 'non-human,' for example, one has to understand – without regard to a superordinated presentation common to both humans and non-humans – everything, without exception, that is not human; hence, angel no less than house, passion, and trumpet blast. Such a conception of the ὄνομα ἀόρσιςτον, however, will hardly be defended these days.

Now, if infinitation really has a dichotomatic effect on a superordinate presentation, then it is clear that expressions like 'non-Greek,' 'non-smoker,' etc. – taken in the discussed sense – far from being meaningless, are justifiedly viewed as categorematic. Infinitation as such, therefore, does not nullify the categorematic nature of an expression. But one sees that this dichotomatic effect of the infinitation is dependent on a condition. There must exist a superordinate presentation for the presentation which is represented by the name which is infinitized. If there is no such presentation, then the infinitized name becomes meaningless. It is clear that 'something' designates a presentation which has no superordinate one; for, if something were superordinate to the something, then the superordinated would also be something; hence, one and the same entity would be superordinated and at the same time also co-ordinated to something else. Infinitation of 'something,' however, presupposes something superordinated to 'something,' and hence something absurd; hence it is not in the same sense possible as, for example, infinitation of names like 'Greek,' etc. Already *Avicenna* pointed this out, and he declared that infinitations like *non-res*, *non-aliquid*, *non-ens* are inadmissible for the reasons here reproduced.[5] And if one takes a closer look at the role which the word 'nothing' plays in language, one finds that this expression is indeed a syncategorematic one and not a name. It is a constituent of negative sentences. 'Nothing is eternal' means 'There is not something which is eternal.' 'I see nothing' means 'There is not something which is seen by me.' Etc.

If these considerations are correct, then the argument for the existence of objectless presentations derived from the expression 'nothing' falls automatically by the wayside, since the expression 'nothing' does not mean a presentation. But it is surprising that the

[5] Compare Prantl, *Geschichte der Logik im Abendland*, vol. 2, p. 356.

syncategorematic nature of this expression escaped a scholar like Bolzano, since he fully recognized the syncategorematic nature of the word 'no.' One can see, he says, that the presentation *no human being* contains the presentations *human being* and *not*, but not at all in such a way that the *not* relates to the presentation *human being* and negates it, but rather this *not* relates to the predicate which comes later in the sentence.[6] And somewhere else Bolzano even talks about the earlier mentioned presupposition for the admission of an infinitation without, however, drawing the appropriate conclusions for the infinitation of *something*.[7]

2 and 3. A second group of allegedly objectless presentations consists of those presentations whose contents combine incompatible characteristics. For example, a presentation of this kind is that of an oblique square. However, a more thorough inspection of the situation shows that those who claim that no object falls under such a presentation are guilty of a confusion. This confusion is easily exposed if one considers the three functions of names; for here, too, we find all three of the functions mentioned earlier, namely, to make known, to mean, and to designate. If someone uses the expression 'oblique square,' then he makes known that there occurs in him an act of presentation. The content, which belongs to this act, constitutes the meaning of this name. But this name does not only mean something, it also designates something, namely, something which combines in itself contradictory properties and whose existence one denies as soon as one feels inclined to make a judgment about it. Something is undoubtedly designated by the name, even though this something does not exist. And what is so designated is different from the content of the presentation; for, firstly, the latter exists, while the former does not, and, secondly, we ascribe properties which are indeed contradictory to what is so designated, but these properties, certainly, do not belong to the content of the presentation. For, if the content had these contradictory properties, then it would not exist; but it does exist. We do not attribute obliqueness and squareness to the content of the presentation, but, rather, whatever is designated by the name 'oblique square' – and what, though it does not exist, is nevertheless presented – is the bearer of these properties. And the oblique square is something presented not in the same sense in which the content is something presented; for the content exists. Rather, the oblique square

[6] Bolzano, *op, cit.*, para. 89, footnote 8.
[7] *Ibid.*, para. 103, footnote.

is something presented in the sense of being the object of the presentation; this object is in this case denied, but it is nevertheless presented as an object. For, only as an object of the presentation can the oblique square be denied; denied is what the name 'oblique square' designates. As content of the presentation, the oblique square cannot be denied; the mental content, which is the meaning of the name, exists in the truest sense of the word.

The confusion of the proponents of objectless presentations consists in that they mistook the nonexistence of an object for its not being presented. But every presentation presents an object, whether it exists or not, just as every name designates an object, regardless of whether the latter exists or not. Although it is, therefore, correct to assert that the objects of certain presentations do not exist, one says too much if one also asserts that no objects fall under these presentations, that these presentations have no objects, that they are objectless.

A weighty objection could be raised against these considerations. One could say that this kind of view obliterates the boundary between existence and nonexistence. The object of a presentation in whose content contradictory characteristics are presented does not exist; yet one asserts that it is presented; hence it exists after all, namely, as a presented object.

If one argues like this, he overlooks the point that if something exists as something presented – in the sense of being the object of a presentation – then this existence is no genuine existence. By means of the additional clause 'as object of a presentation,' the meaning of the expression 'existence' is modified; something which exists as an object of a presentation does in truth not exist at all, but is merely presented. Opposed to the real existence of an object – as it constitutes the content of a judgment of affirmation – is the phenomenal, intentional existence of this object; the latter consists entirely in its being presented.[8] Far from obliterating the boundary between existence and nonexistence, our earlier considerations rather contribute to a sharpening of this boundary. For now we know that one must beware of confusing the existence of an object with its being presented. The latter as little involves and establishes the existence of the object presented as an object's being designated presupposes or results in its existence. Scholasticism recognized quite clearly the peculiar status of objects which are presented but do not exist, and it coined the

[8] Compare Brentano, *op. cit.*, vol. 2, chapter 1, para. 7.

expression that these objects have only objective, intentional existence, while being well aware that one does not designate true existence by this expression. However, their discussion did confine itself to possible objects, objects free of contradiction, and left out impossible objects. But there is no obvious reason why whatever holds for the former should not also be applicable to the latter. If one is presented with a nonexisting object, one does not always have to notice on first glance whether or not the object has contradictory determinations. It is conceivable that the determinations of these objects appear at first to be quite compatible and only prove to be incompatible in the light of further consequences. In this case, the presentation would have an object as long as these contradictions go unnoticed; but at the very moment at which one becomes aware of them, the presentation would cease to have an object. What, then, would have these contradictory properties? Surely, not the content; for the contradictory determinations are presented in it, but do not belong to it. Hence no other alternative remains but that these determinations are presented as belonging to the object; and, surely, the object itself must then be presented.

The difference between presentations with possible and presentations with impossible objects consists in the fact that the person has in the first case, when he has a presentation of something possible, generally much less occasion to make a judgment of affirmation or denial about this non-contradictory object than in the second case when he has a presentation of an impossible object and is aware of its impossibility. In this second case, almost inevitably a judgment of denial will occur, and it will be difficult not to make this judgment. But even though one is immediately inclined to deny the object and, by following this inclination, one makes the judgment *This object does not exist*, nevertheless, in order to make this judgment, one must have a presentation of the object.

The doctrine of true and false presentations as it still appears in Descartes and his successors remains incomprehensible without the presupposition that to every presentation without exception there corresponds an object. Every presentation, according to Descartes, presents something as an object. Now, if this object exists, then the presentation is materially true; if it does not exist, then the idea is materially false.[9]

[9] Descartes, *Meditationes de prima philosophia*, Med. III: Nullae ideae nisi tamquam rerum esse possunt. – Est tamen profecta quaedam alia falsitas materialis in ideis, cum non rem tamquam rem repraesentant.

It is obviously Descartes' view that, irrespective of whether the object exists or not, it is always presented through the presentation. The question is only whether there corresponds to this intentional existence of the object in the presentation a true existence; and in presenting the really existing objects as well as the merely intentionally existing objects indiscriminately in the same way, the presentation easily leads to false judgments, since one can be as inclined to believe that the merely intentionally existing objects truly exist as that the really existing objects exist.

We thus find in Descartes a confirmation of our view that to every presentation there corresponds an object. If we have successfully shown that even those presentations have objects in whose content contradictory determinations are presented, then a corresponding proof has also been given for the third group of allegedly "objectless" presentations, namely, presentations whose objects, though they are not impossible, are such that their existence is as a matter of fact not given in experience. We shall, therefore, maintain that every presentation presents an object, whether the object exists or not. Even presentations whose objects *cannot* exist are no exception to this law.

The fact that to every act and content of a presentation there belongs necessarily an object sheds clear light on the nature of the peculiar relationship between the mental act – which we call being presented – and its object. For, the relation to an object which is characteristic of the class of presentations is distinguished from the relation characteristic of judgments in the following way, namely, in that the latter always concerns the existence or nonexistence of an object, while the object is simply presented by the former class of mental phenomena, regardless of whether the object exists or not.

It is not surprising that we assert here relations which are such that one of their terms exists, while the other does not – and hence relations between existents and nonexistents – if one considers that the question of whether the terms of a relation exist or do not exist is completely irrelevant so far as the relation which "obtains" between them is concerned, as Hoefler has shown.[10] He does, however, make the mistake of confusing the content with the object of the presentation. He says: A judgment which asserts a relation does not assume a "real" existence of the terms of the relation; it is sufficient to have a presentation of these terms, and the judgment then concerns these contents. This seems to be incorrect in as much as the contents of pre-

[10] *Op. cit.*, para. 45, II.

sentations do exist, but do not constitute the terms of the relation which is asserted in the judgment. If one says that the number four is greater than the number three, then one does not talk about a relation between the content of the presentation of three and the content of the presentation of four; for there are no relations of magnitude between contents. Rather, the relation occurs between "the number three" and "the number four," both taken as objects of presentations, regardless of whether they exist or not, if they are only presented *through* corresponding presentations.

If this is so, then there arises another difficulty which was already pointed out by Hoefler. Relation-judgments which are about the existence of a relation between nonexisting objects seem to affirm the objects themselves; and according to what was said earlier about the relationship between the affirmation of parts and the affirmation of the whole containing these parts, the affirmation of a relation must involve the affirmation of every term of this relation. This consideration thus leads to a conclusion which directly contradicts the assertion that the existence of relation-terms does not matter for a relation-judgment. But this difficulty disappears because of the following observations.

According to the idiogenetic theory of judgment – that is, the theory which sees the nature of judgment in the affirmation or denial of an object – there are only particular affirmative and general negative judgments.[11] So-called general affirmative and particular negative judgments can be reduced to these two classes.[12] Now, in regard to general negative relation-judgments, the just mentioned difficulty does not really exist. Such a judgment, for example, There is no circle with unequal radii (expressed categorically: All radii of a circle are equal to each other) – does not contain anything about the existence of the radii. It merely denies the inequality of the radii of a circle without asserting something about the existence of the radii themselves. In regard to particular affirmative judgments which assert something about a relation, the aformentioned difficulty disappears when one considers the true subject of such sentences. By means of the sentence 'Poseidon was the god of the sea' we seem to affirm implicitly Poseidon himself through an affirmation of the relationship between Poseidon and the sea. But this is mere appearance; for, since the proper name supposits – in the terminology of the scholastics – in

[11] Hillebrand, *op. cit.*, para. 16.
[12] Brentano, *op. cit.*, vol. II, ch. 7, para. 7.

this case for the designated entity as something designated, the subject of the sentence is not 'Poseidon,' but 'something called Poseidon.'[13] Hence, what is implicitly affirmed is something designated as designated, an object of a presentation inasmuch as it is designated, not the plain object of the presentation.

We have therefore shown that the relationship between the act of presentation and the corresponding object is independent of the question of whether or not this object exists. Hence nothing stands in the way of asserting that to every presentation there corresponds an object, whether the object exists or not. The expression 'objectless presentation' is such that it contains a contradiction; for, there is no presentation which does not present something as an object; there can be no such presentation. But there are many presentations whose objects do not exist, either because the objects combine contradictory determinations and hence cannot exist, or because they simply do in fact not exist. Yet in all such cases an object is presented, so that one may speak of presentations whose objects do not exist, but not of presentations which are objectless, of presentations to which no object corresponds.[14]

[13] Compare Marty: "Ueber subjectlose Saetze etc." *Vierteljahrsschrift fuer wissenschaftliche Philosophie*, vol. 8, p. 82; and Hillebrand, *op. cit.*, para. 68, footnote.

[14] By the way, Bolzano is forced to deal in a special paragraph with the question of how the relationships which hold for presentations with objects (for example, the relation between equivalent ideas, relationships of sub- and superordination) can be extended to "objectless" presentations. – We find in Kerry, too, a statement which confirms – perhaps without the author's intention – our view. He says: "The proposition: 'There is no equilateral plane triangle with unequal angles' shows clearly that one can somehow think (though, of course, not in an intuitive way [*anschaulich*]) of the object whose existence is here negated." *Op. cit.*, 9, p. 472.

# 6. THE DIFFERENCE BETWEEN CONTENT AND OBJECT

That the content and the object of a presentation are different from each other will hardly be denied when the object exists. If one says, 'The sun exists,' one obviously does not mean the content of one's presentation of the sun, but rather something which is totally different from this content. The case is not so simple for presentations whose objects do *not* exist. It is tempting to believe that in this case there is no real difference between content and object, but only a logical one; that in this case content and object are really one; and that this one entity appears sometimes as content, sometimes as object, because of the two points of view from which one can look at it.

But this is not so. To the contrary, a brief consideration shows that the differences between content and object of a presentation which can be ascertained when the object exists also are present when the object does not exist. We shall list the most important of these differences and try to show for each one how it occurs for existing as well as nonexisting objects.

1. In order to prove the existence of the difference under discussion, we have already repeatedly called attention to the entirely different ways in which content and object behave in regard to affirmative and negative judgments. Namely, if the content and the object of a presentation were not really but only logically different, then it would not be possible, say, for the content to exist while the object does not exist. But this often happens. If one makes a true judgment which denies an object, then one must surely have a presentation of the object which one judges and denies. The object is therefore presented as an object by means of a corresponding content. Whenever this is the case, the content exists, but the object does not exist; for it is this object which is denied in a true negative judgment. If content and object were really the same, then it would be impossible for the one to exist and for the other at the same time not to exist. Hence, we

derive the most effective argument for a real difference between the content and the object of a presentation from this relationship between the true, denying judgment, on the one hand, and the object and content of the presentation on which the judgment is based, on the other.

2. Kerry mentions another argument. He says that the difference between the concept of a number and the number itself can be seen because of the fact that the number has properties and stands in relations which are completely alien to its concept.[1] Kerry understands by the concept what we call the content of a presentation; the number itself is the object. For example, a golden mountain has among others the properties of being spatially extended, of consisting of gold, of being larger than other mountains. These properties and the relation to other mountains obviously do not belong to the content of the presentation of a golden mountain; for the latter is neither spatially extended, nor does it consist of gold, nor do propositions about relations of magnitude apply to it. And even though the golden mountain does not exist, one ascribes to it, insofar as it is an object of a presentation, these properties, and one relates it to other objects of presentations which perhaps do not exist either. And the same holds for objects to which one attributes contradictory determinations. These contradictory determinations are not attributed to the content. The content of the presentation of an oblique square is neither oblique nor square; rather, the oblique square, the object of this presentation, has these properties. From this viewpoint, too, there appears a difference between the content and the object of presentations.

Liebmann, who endeavors to distinguish very sharply between the act and the content of presentations as completely different entities, overlooks the difference between the content and the object. He says: "The contents of our visual and tactual presentations always possess, together with spatial extension, certain geometric predicates like position, shape, etc. The *having* of this content, however, is as inaccessible to these geometric predicates as brightness, strength of tone, temperature, and other intensive magnitudes."[2] Liebmann here calls "content" what we call "object" of a presentation; for the latter possessses the geometric predicates mentioned by Liebmann. However, if Liebmann understands by content what we call object, then his remarks, though correct, fail to mention that link between the act and

[1] Kerry, *op. cit.*, vol. 10, p. 428.

[2] Liebmann, *Zur Analyse der Wirklichkeit* (Strassburg, 1876), p. 15.

the object of a presentation by means of which an act intends this particular and no other object. And this link, the content in our sense, is not the same as the act. It does form together with the act one single mental reality, but while the act of having a presentation is something real, the content of the presentation always lacks reality. The object sometimes has reality, sometimes not. This different behavior in regard to the property of being real, too, reflects the difference between the content and the object of a presentation.

3. A further proof for the real, not merely logical, difference between the content and the object of a presentation follows from the existence of so-called equivalent presentations [*Wechselvorstellungen*]. According to the customary definition, such presentations have the same extension but different contents. An example of equivalent presentations is: *the city located at the site of the Roman Juvavum* and *the birthplace of Mozart*. These two names have a different meaning, but they both designate the same thing. Now, since the meaning of a name, as we saw, coincides with the content of the presentation designated by the name, and since what the name names is the object of the presentation, we can also define equivalent presentations as presentations *in* which a different content, but *through* which the same object, is presented. But the difference between content and object is thereby already given. For one conceives of something quite different when conceiving of the city which is located at the site of the Roman Juvavum from what one conceives of when conceiving of the birthplace of Mozart. These two presentations consist of very different parts. The first contains as parts the presentations of Romans and of an ancient city forming a fortified camp; the second presentation contains as parts the presentations of a composer and of the relation in which he stands to his native city, while the relation to an old settlement formerly occupying that site, which was presented by the first presentation, is absent. In spite of these great differences between the parts of the contents both contents intend one and the same object. The same properties which belong to Mozart's birthplace also belong to the city located at the former site of the Roman Juvavum; the latter is identical with Mozart's birthplace. The object of the presentation is the same; what distinguishes them are their different contents.

These considerations can be easily applied to presentations whose objects do not exist. Admittedly, a circle in the strict geometric sense does not exist anywhere. Yet one can conceive of it in different ways, be it as a line of constant curvature, be it as a figure expressed by the equation $(x-a)^2 + (y-b)^2 = r^2$, be it as a line whose points are at the same distance from a given point. All these different presentations intend the same. The one thing which they all intend is their object; what distinguishes them from each other is their contents.

This argument from equivalent presentations is not so easily applied to the real difference between content and object of presentations whose objects contain contradictory determinations. If one conceives of an oblique square and of a square with unequal diagonals, then one has – as is the case for all equivalent presentations – two presentations with partly the same and partly different contents. But whether or not these different contents intend the *same* object is hard to determine, because there are no other presentations of the object except the equivalent presentations, and hence what Kerry calls "acquaintance" [*Kenntnisnahme*] with the object is impossible.[3] A comparison between the properties of the object of one of the equivalent presentations and the properties of the object of the other equivalent presentation is, moreover, impossible, because every logical connection among the characteristics is abolished. However, a substitute for this way of determining identity of object for equivalent presentations is at hand:

One can form the presentation of an object with contradictory determinations whose content presents more than just a single pair of such contradictory determinations; for example, the presentation of a square, oblique figure with unequal diagonals. Here the determinations *square* and *oblique* as well as the determinations *square* and *having unequal diagonals* contradict each other in pairs. The presentation which has both pairs as content presents a single, nonexisting object. But one can now divide this presentation into two by conceiving each time of only one of the two contradictory pairs of properties. One can conceive at one time of the square, oblique figure with unequal diagonals by conceiving only of the determinations *square* and *oblique*, and the other time one can conceive of the same object, which by assumption is square and oblique, by conceiving merely of the pair of properties designated by the words: "being square with unequal diagonals." According to the assumption, one conceives of the same object through both presentations, but these presentations have only partially the same content and, hence, are genuine equivalent presentations. In this way, the argument from equivalent presentations for the difference between content and object can also be applied to

[3] Kerry, *op. cit.*, vol. 15, p. 160.

presentations whose objects cannot exist, because single determinations of these objects are incompatible with each other.

4. Kerry uses a further argument in order to prove that content and object are not identical. A general presentation as a presentation under which a *plurality of objects* falls has nevertheless only *a single content* and thus proves that content and object have to be sharply distinguished.[4] This argument is, as it were, a complement to the earlier one according to which the very same difference between content and object follows from the fact that several contents correspond to a single object. However, that a plurality of objects falls under a general presentation seems to be a mistaken view – as shocking as this may sound – and therefore Kerry's argument which is based on this view seems to be untenable.

Yet even without this argument, the reasons listed above seem to show sufficiently that one has to distinguish between content and object of a presentation even if this object must be denied.

[4] Kerry, *op. cit.*, vol. 10, p. 432.

## 7. DESCRIPTION OF THE OBJECT OF A PRESENTATION

In calling what is presented by a presentation its object, we give a meaning to this word which Kant had already attached to it. "The highest concept," he writes, "with which one usually begins a transcendental philosophy, is the division into what is possible and what is impossible. However, since all division presupposes a concept which is to be divided, an even higher concept must be mentioned, and this is the concept of an object in general [*ueberhaupt*] (taken in a problematic sense and leaving open whether it is something or nothing.)"[1] We have to modify the sense which Kant attaches to the word 'object' in only one respect. According to Kant, the object can be "something" or "nothing." We have already said earlier (p. 19f.), in contrast to Kant, that 'nothing' cannot be taken to be a name for objects of possible presentations, but must be viewed as a syncategorematic expression: 'nothing' marks the limit of presentation, where it ceases to be presentation. We may add to the reasons already mentioned for this conception of "nothing" the following reason. We have called object that entity which is presented through a presentation, judged in a judgment, and desired or detested in an emotion. If "nothing" were the object of a presentation, then it should be possible to affirm or deny it in a judgment, to desire or detest it. But this is not at all the case. One can say neither *"Nothing" exists* nor *"Nothing" does not exist*, and one can neither desire "nothing" nor detest it. If one nevertheless uses these or similar phrases, then the expression 'nothing' either reveals quite openly its syncategorematic nature – as when the solipsist says *There is nothing* = there is not something real outside of the subject – or it stands, as it were, figuratively for another name, as when the Buddhist says that death is followed by a condition of nothing.

[1] Kant, *op. cit.*, p. 259.

Hence, if one says one has a presentation of nothing, then one does not have a presentation of anything; if one has a presentation, then one has a presentation of something, of an object.

Bolzano and Erdmann follow Kant in regard to this use of the word 'object'; both admit "nothing" as a kind of object.[2] So does Kerry.[3] But he finds fault with the Kantian use of the word 'object' in a different direction. He maintains that Kant uses this word not always in the same sense; sometimes, the object is said to be a real object "affecting the mind," at other times, it is the object of a concept.[4] In regard to this question, we want to make our point of view precise without investigating whether Kerry's reproach of Kant is justified.

According to our view, the object of presentations, of judgments, of feelings, as well as of volitions, is something different from the thing as such [*Ding an sich*], if we understand by the latter the unknown cause of what affects our senses. The meaning of the word 'object' coincides in this respect with the meaning of the expression 'phenomenon' or 'appearance,' whose cause is either, according to Berkeley, God, or, according to the extreme idealists, our own mind, or, according to the moderate "real-idealists," the respective things as such. What we have said so far about the objects of presentation and what will come to light about them in the following investigations is claimed to hold no matter which one of the just mentioned viewpoints one may choose. Every presentation presents something, no matter whether it exists or not, no matter whether it appears as independent of us and forces itself upon our perception, or whether it is formed by us in our own imagination; whatever it may be, it is – insofar as we have a presentation of it – the object of these acts, in contrast to us and our activity of conceiving.

Whether this object is something real or unreal will be difficult to decide as long as there is no agreement about the meaning of these expressions. The reality of an object has nothing to do with its existence. An object is said to be something real or not, regardless of whether it exists or not, just as one can talk about the simplicity or complexity of an object without asking whether it exists or not. In what the reality of an object consists, cannot be expressed in words; but most philosophers seem to agree nowadays that objects like a

[2] Bolzano, *op. cit.*, para. 49, 1. And Erdmann, "Zur Theorie der Apperception," *Vierteljahrsschrift fuer wissenschaftliche Philosophie*, 10, pp. 313 ff., and *Logik*, vol. 1, para. 8–34, especially para. 15.

[3] *Op. cit.*, vol. 13, p. 122, footnote.

[4] *Ibid.*, vol. 10, p. 464, footnote.

piercing tone, a tree, grief, motion, are something real, while objects like lack, absence, possibility, etc. are to count as *not* real.[5] Now, just as a real object may either exist or not exist, so, too, can something nonreal either exist or not exist. Judgments like: There exists a lack of money, or: There is no possibility that this or that will happen, are true or false completely independently of the nonreality of the object which is affirmed or denied by them.

Thus we reply to Kerry's reproach of Kant that it is entirely possible, taking the word 'object' in the sense here adopted, to speak either of a real object or of the object of a concept – a nonreal object – since objects, just as they can be divided into existing and nonexisting objects, can also be divided into those that are real and those that are not.

There is still another expression in regard to which we must fix the meaning of the word 'object.' The latter must not be confused with "subjects" [*Sachen*] or "things" [*Dingen*]. These form only one group of objects; there are many other objects which are neither subjects nor things. To the objects belong *all* categories of what is conceivable, while subjects or things constitute only *one* of these categories. A deadly fall is not a thing, but it is nevertheless an object like, for example, experiment, murder, epileptic fit, peace of mind, sine (in trigonometry), etc.

In order to explain the meaning of the word 'object' further, one can also – as we have done already – point to the linguistic designation and assert that everything which is designated is an object. Such a designation uses either *nomina* understood in a grammatical sense, or it uses phrases consisting of *nomina* and other expressions, or, finally, it uses other parts of speech, assuming that they have been converted into nouns. One can, therefore, say that everything which is designated by a noun or by an expression which is used as a noun is an object in the sense here adopted.

Now, since everything can be object – object of presentation – the subject of the presentation itself not excluded, those who conceive of the object as the *summum genus* are justified. Everything which is, is an object of a possible presentation; everything which is, is something. And here, therefore, is the point where the psychological discussion of the difference between content and object of presentations turns into metaphysics.

[5] Marty, *op. cit.*, vol. 8, pp. 171 ff.

The objects of presentations have indeed been viewed from a metaphysical point of view up to the present time. In calling them ὄντα, *entia*, one revealed the way which led to them. However, that the Aristotelian ὄν – like the *ens* of medieval philosophy – is nothing else but the object of presentations is shown by the fact that all doctrines about the *ens*, as far as they are correct, hold for the object of presentations. We shall confine ourselves here to the most famous of these doctrines.

1. The object is something different from the existent; some objects have existence in addition to their objecthood [*Gegenstaendlichkeit*], that is, in addition to their property of being presented (which is the real sense of the word '*essentia*'); others do not. What exists is an object (*ens habens actualem existentiam*), as is also what merely could exist (*ens possibile*); even what never can exist but what can only be conceived of (*ens rationis*) is an object; in short, everything which is not nothing, but which in some sense is "something," is an object.[6] In fact, the majority of scholastics maintain that "*aliquid*" is synonymous with "*ens*," in contrast to those who conceive of the former as an attribute of the latter.

2. Object is *summum genus*. Scholastics express this by the statement that the concept of *ens* is not a generic concept, but is a transcendental concept, because it "*omnia genera transcendit.*"

3. Every object of a presentation can be object of a judgment and object of an emotion. This is the meaning of the scholastic doctrine that every object of a presentation is "true" and "good." The (metaphysical) truth of an object does not consist in being judged in a (logically) true judgment; as little as its "goodness" depends on whether the feeling concerning it is good in the ethical sense or not. Rather, an object is called true inasmuch as it is object of a judgment, and it is called good inasmuch as it is related to an emotion. To be sure, the scholastics do not always strictly adhere to this meaning of the truth and goodness of an object. For example, if one defines metaphysical truth as the "*conformitas inter rem et intellectum*," then one presupposes the truth of the judgment about the respective object. And when Thomas Aquinas, for example, sees the truth of an object in its "*cognoscibilitas*" or "*intelligibilitas*," then a regard for the truth of the judgment is included; for every piece of knowledge is a true judgment

[6] Some philosophers, like Suarez, withhold the name *ens* from what has merely a "*ficta*" or "*chimaerica essentia*" and give it only to the "*essentia realis.*" However, this restriction seems to involve an inconsistency. Suarez, *Disputationes metaphysicae* II, sect. 4.

And yet Thomas abandons this view when he teaches: "*Sicut bonum nominat id, in quod tendit appetitus, ita verum nominat id, in quod tendit intellectus.*"[7] This version of the doctrine amounts to nothing else but that an object is called true in that it is intended by a judgment and that it is called good in that it is intended by a feeling. And since every object can be subjected to a judgment, to a desire or abhorrence, truth and goodness belong to every object of a presentation, and the scholastic doctrine proves correct in the sense that every *ens* is *verum* as well as *bonum*.

4. An object is called true with regard to its ability to be judged; it is called good with regard to its ability to be the object of an emotion. The question could be raised whether the object has, in an analogical manner, an attribute which expresses its conceivability and which, therefore, would be a name of the object inasmuch as it is presented. Now, medieval philosophy knows of a third attribute of the object; every *ens*, according to this philosophy, is not only *verum* and *bonum*, but also *unum*. We shall investigate in a different context – since this question will arise there quite naturally – what this unity means for the presentation of an object, especially whether we may see in it the analogue in the sphere of presentations to truth in the sphere of judgments and goodness in the sphere of emotions.

5. If the object of presentations, judgments, and feelings is nothing else but the Aristotelian-scholastic *ens*, then metaphysics must be definable as the science of objects in general, taking this word in the sense here proposed. And this is indeed the case. The particular sciences, too, deal with nothing else but the objects of our presentations, their changes, their properties, as well as the laws according to which objects affect each other. Only, the particular sciences always deal with a more or less limited group of objects, a group which is formed by the natural context or a certain purpose. The natural sciences, in the widest sense of the word, for example, are concerned with the peculiarities of those objects which one calls inorganic and organic bodies; psychology investigates the properties and laws characteristic of mental phenomena, of mental objects. Metaphysics is a science which considers all objects, physical – organic and inorganic – as well as mental, real as well as nonreal, existing objects as well as nonexisting objects; investigates those laws which objects in general obey, not just a certain group of objects. What we here mean is

[7] Thomas Acquinas, *De veritate*, pars 1, quaest. 16, art. 1.

expressed by the venerable definition of metaphysics as the science of being [*Seienden*] as such.[8]

The backward glance at some of the points of the scholastic doctrine of *ens* is supposed to characterize as precisely as possible the meaning which we connect, in the present investigation, with the word 'object.' Summarizing what was said, we can describe the object in the following way. Everything that is presented through a presentation, that is affirmed or denied through a judgment, that is desired or detested through an emotion, we call an object. Objects are either real or not real; they are either possible or impossible objects; they exist or do not exist. What is common to them all is that they are or that they can be the *object* (*not* the intentional one!) of mental acts, that their linguistic designation is the name (in the sense defined above on p. 9), and that considered as *genus*, they form the *summum genus* which finds its usual linguistic expression in the word 'something.' Everything which is in the widest sense "something" is called "object," first of all in regard to a subject, but then also regardless of this relationship.

[8] Compare Brentano, *op. cit.*, vol. 1, chapter 1, para. 1.

# 8. THE AMBIGUITY OF THE TERM 'CHARACTERISTIC'

If we have succeeded in showing that the object of a presentation is in fact different from its content, then it follows that the parts of a content must also be different from the parts of the presented object. Hence, since it can only be confusing when one takes at times the intentional object – thus the content – at other times, the real object as the object of a presentation, and since this confusion does in fact occur in some philosophers, there exists, as a result of that misleading terminology, a twofold use of the word 'characteristic,' which is applied at times to the intentional object, hence to the content, at other times to the object.

*Kerry*, for example, speaks of concepts which are such that their content and their object "contain strictly the same characteristics."[1] According to *Harms*, the concept consists of the enduring characteristics of a thing.[2] Marty, too, thinks of a concept as being formed from the characteristics of an object.[3] These scholars thus use the word 'characteristic' for the parts of an object as well as for the parts of a content of a presentation. And they are not the only ones.[4]

But if content and object are not identical with each other, then their parts are also different; hence they can only be equivocally designated by one and the same expression. For this reason *Hoppe* protested against a scientific use of the word 'characteristic.' Despite its frequent use in logic, this expression seems to him to be unsuited as a *terminus technicus* and to be an ordinary word which has been transferred to science.[5] And he seems to be right if one considers that even scholars who, according to their most explicit assurance, mean by 'characteris-

[1] *Op. cit.*, vol. 10, p. 424.
[2] Harms, *Logik*, publ. by v. Wiese (Leipzig, 1886), p. 196.
[3] *Op. cit.*, vol. 8, p. 82.
[4] Compare Schroeder, *Algebra der Logik*, vol. 1, pp. 57 f., 80 f., 91 ff.; Gutberlet, *Lehrbuch der Philosophie*, p. 10 and other places.
[5] Hoppe, *Die gesammte Logik* (Paderborn, 1868), para. 104, 111 f.

tics' parts of the contents of presentations, call also, without further ado, properties of the object of a presentation a characteristic. Sigwart calls the elements or partial presentations of which complex presentations consist characteristics. Nevertheless, he counts as characteristics color, equality of the sides, extension, etc.; and yet Sigwart surely does not want to maintain that the presentation of a triangle is composed of a certain color, an extension, etc.; for, otherwise, this presentation (that is, the content of the presentation) would be something extended, colored, etc.[6] Hoefler, who explicitly defines characteristics as those constituents of a content which are presentations of the properties of an object, almost in the same breath calls these properties themselves characteristics and speaks of the "characteristic whiteness" and the "characteristic color," while he really only allows us to call the presentations of whiteness, etc. characteristics.[7] – Baumann calls everything a partial presentation or characteristic which can be distinguished in a complex presentation; the content of a presentation is, therefore, nothing else but the totality of its characteristics conceived of as a whole. Yet he lists as examples of characteristics: heavy, extensible, shiny, etc.[8] This ambiguity of the word 'characteristic' is a result of the fact that the content and the object of a presentation are not strictly distinguished. Had one always made this distinction, then one would not have overlooked the difference between the two meanings of the word 'presented' and, consequently, would not have designated by the same name the parts of what is presented in one sense, the content, and the parts of what is presented in the other sense, the object.

Just as the whole object is presented through a presentation, so the single parts of the object are presented through corresponding parts of the presentation. Now, the parts of the object of a presentation are again objects of presentation, and the latter in turn are parts of the whole presentation. Parts of the content of a presentation are contents, just as parts of an object are objects. In analogy to the way in which parts of an object form the whole uniform object, parts of a content form the complete content.

Hence, if one, for example, has a presentation of an apple, one also has presentations of its parts. The apple as well as its parts are presented; the apple is the whole, uniform object; its parts are partial objects to which there correspond certain definite parts of the content of

[6] Sigwart, *op. cit.*, vol. 1, para. 41 f.
[7] Hoefler, *op. cit.*, para. 15. 1.
[8] Baumann, *Einleitung in die Philosophie*, pp. 9 f.

the presentation which intends the apple. But when the apple and its parts are presented, by being so presented they do not cease being objects of a presentation. As little as the apple turns into a presentation when one has a presentation of it, as little do the parts of the apple turn into parts of the content of the presentation just because they are presented. For "to be presented" means here something like: to be an object of a presentation; it is the term in its determining meaning. "The apple is presented" means nothing else but that the apple enters into a certain relationship with a being capable of having presentations. Hence, if one understands by 'characteristics' parts of an object, then one is fully justified in speaking of presented characteristics; one must only keep in mind that "to be presented" means here "to be object of a presentation," and that, therefore, the characteristic which is presented in this sense is not a part of a presentation, but rather is a part of the object of a presentation.

People seem to have overlooked this very point when they substituted – without being fully aware of it – the modifying sense of the word 'presented' for its determining sense. The presented apple and the presentation of the apple seemed to be the same in every case, while this sameness only obtains between the meanings of the two expressions if one takes 'presented' in the modifying sense, that is, if one means by the presented apple the content of the presentation of the apple; for the latter, too, is presented. Of course, the presented apple in this sense is not an apple, but the content of a presentation. In this way, the parts of the apple which one called characteristics turned into parts of the content, since one meant by the presented apple the content of the presentation of the apple. The characteristic as a part of the apple is turned into a part of the content; for the *content* of the presentation was the presented apple. And if it was this content, then the presented parts of the apple were parts of the content of the presentation.

Hence, just as one understood by 'what is presented' sometimes the content, at other times the object of a presentation, so one meant by 'characteristic' – designated by this word parts of 'what is presented' – sometimes parts of the content, at other times parts of the object. And since many philosophers did not sufficiently or did not all distinguish between content and object, thinking of them as one and the same thing, they also designated with the same name 'characteristic' parts of the one, of the content, and parts of the other, of the object.

That these observations are not unfounded is shown by Sigwart's exposition of the traditional view about the composition of concepts.

Sigwart does not approve of this view at all; he merely summarizes it, for the purpose of criticism, as follows: "The traditional view about concepts teaches how to determine by means of characteristics what is conceived through a uniform presentation which is designated by a single word, how to analyze a concept into its partial presentations or partial concepts. These are thought *in* the concept and constitute its content. Thus in the concept gold, the characteristics heavy, yellow, shiny, metallic, etc. are thought; in the concept square, the characreristics bounded, foursided, equilateral, rectangular, plane figure; in the concept murder, the characteristics illegal, intentional, deliberate killing of a human being. The totality of these characteristics constitutes the content of the concepts gold, square, and murder; and one conceives of this content, I suppose, as the sum or the product of the single characteristics."[9]

Sigwart thus reports that "what is determined through characteristics" is "what is thought of" through a uniform presentation, which is designated by a single word. Apart from the fact that something may well be thought of through a uniform presentation without being designated by *one* word, we find here the already criticized ambiguity in the use of 'what is presented'; an ambiguity which is not eliminated by an apparent substitution of the expression 'what is thought of' for 'what is presented.' For what is determined by characteristics is either the object or the content of a presentation. According to the examples mentioned by Sigwart, it is the object which is determined by the characteristics; for it is not the content of the presentation of gold, but rather the gold itself as the object of the presentation, which has the determinations heavy, yellow, shiny, metallic, etc. The determinations are presented *through* the presentation of gold; but the totality of these determinations does not constitute the content of the presentation of gold. Rather, the latter consists of as many (or even more) parts as there are determinations of gold which are presented through parts of that total presentation and which are, hence, also presented through presentations. The content of the presentation of gold, therefore, does not consist of the totality of characteristics, but of the totality of presentations of these characteristics.

In his discussion of this doctrine of traditional logic, Sigwart himself overlooks the ambiguity of the expression 'something is something thought of,' an ambiguity which we try to avoid by means of the distinction between what is thought *in* a presentation (hence as content)

[9] Sigwart, *op. cit.*, vol. 1, para. 41.

and what is thought *through* a presentation (hence as object). If Sigwart had noticed this ambiguity, then he would not have cited Ueberweg's definition of the characteristic as confirming his exposition of the traditional view about concepts; for it is Ueberweg who explicitly calls attention to the fact that it will not do to talk about the characteristic sometimes as a part of a content, sometimes as a part of a presentation. He says, in this context: "Characteristic (*nota*, τεχμήριον) of an object is everything which distinguishes it from other objects. The presentation of a characteristic is contained in the presentation of the object as a partial presentation, that is, as a part of the whole presentation (*repraesentatio particularis*). Characteristics are characteristics of the thing [Sache], of the real object, or, at least, of the object which is presented as if it were real. One is only justified in speaking of the characteristics of a presentation, inasmuch as the presentation itself is conceived of as something objective, that is, as object of a thought. 'To incorporate a characteristic into a presentation' is an abbreviation for 'to become aware of a characteristic of a thing by means of the corresponding partial presentation' or for 'to incorporate into the presentation an element through which the respective characterization of the thing is presented.'"[10]

A more welcome confirmation of what we have said is hardly conceivable. According to Ueberweg, too, the characteristic is a part of an object, and just as the object is presented though the whole presentation, so the simple parts of this object are presented *through* single parts of the whole presentation. However, what is presented *in* the whole presentation are, as it were, the parts of this whole presentation, the partial presentation whose "totality – interconnected in a way which is determined by the respective real relationships – forms the content (*complexus*) of a presentation."

But Ueberweg is not the only one we can call upon to back us up. Bolzano, who uses the word 'characteristic' in a much narrower sense than Ueberweg, strongly objects to the ambiguous use of this expression according to which it means sometimes, part of a content, sometimes, part of an object. He says: "It had been recognized that not every characteristic of an object is conceived of through the presentation of the object; hence one arrived here at the concept of something which is thought through a presentation simultaneously with other things, and it would now have been necessary to find a fitting term for this

[10] Ueberweg, *System der Logik*, edit. and publ. by Juergen Bona Meyer (Bonn, 1882), para. 49 f.

concept. In my opinion, such a term would have been the expression 'part of constituent or a presentation.' However, this term was used only very rarely; rather, people preferred to call those characteristics 'essential,' 'original,' or also 'constitutive' characteristics. Now, as good as this last term is, it favors only too well the notion that a concept is nothing else but the totality of certain characteristics which constitute it, that is, that there are no other constituents of a concept (or of a presentation in general) than characteristics." If one now also permits oneself – supposedly for the sole purpose of convenience – to call the characteristics of the object of a presentation characteristics of this concept itself, then this, too, contributes to a confusion between the characteristics of an object – as long as they are necessary – and the constituents of a concept."[11]

Thus, what Ueberweg attributes to a desire to be concise, Bolzano blames on convenience, namely, the fact that people saw fit to give one and the same name to both the constituents of the object and the constituents of the content of a presentation. Bolzano considers the question of whether one is correct in doing this so important that he talks about the matter not only at the place mentioned above, but returns to it repeatedly.[12] This fact as well as the fact that a strict distinction between the characteristic as something which belongs to the object of a presentation, on the one hand, and as a constituent of the content of a presentation, on the other, has important consequences – as will appear – justifies our dwelling on this question, even though it may look like a mere terminological matter at first glance. We can lay down as a result of our considerations that only the parts of the object of a presentation are to be called characteristics, never the parts of the content of a presentation. We shall take up later the question of what parts of an object can be called characteristics and what parts cannot. (See chapter 13).

Since we reserve the expression 'characteristic' for parts of the object of a presentation, we have to produce a term for the parts of the content of a presentation. It is customary to call these parts partial presentations. But there are objections to this custom. Sigwart maintains that the term 'partial concept' or 'partial presentation,' being derived from spatial or temporal relationships, can only be used figuratively; for, partial presentations are not supposed to be presentations of the parts of a whole (for example, of a head, neck, body, etc. as parts of an

[11] Bolzano, *op. cit.*, para. 65, 11.
[12] *Ibid.*, para. 89, footnote 5, and para. 112, footnote.

animal) which stand to the presentation of the whole in the same relation in which the parts stand to the whole, but rather are supposed to be constituents of the presentation in the way that the single properties are constituents of a thing.[13]

Now, whether or not partial presentations are presentations of the parts of a whole will be decided later on. But the term 'partial presentations' as a term for the constituents of the content of a presentation, already proves inadequate for another more obvious reason. To see this, one merely has to reflect that not only the relatively more simple contents of a presentation into which it can be analyzed belong to the constituents of the content of the presentation, but that the relations among these relatively more simple constituents also belong as constituents – though of a different kind – to the total content. And these relations which are not at all presentations can hardly be called partial presentations. Lotze is therefore right when he asserts that it is "a drawback that we lack an adequate term for the constituents out of which we compose the concept; 'characteristic' and 'partial presentation,' fit only in certain cases."[14]

In order to eliminate this drawback, one can use the expression 'element' for the constituents of the content of a presentation. This term is suited both for those constituents of the content which in turn are contents of a presentation as well as for those which are not. Contemporary scholars like Wundt show a special preference for the use of this term in the sense just explained. However, it may be expedient to save this expression for those components of the mental life which cannot be further decomposed by psychological analysis; thus allowing it to have part of that meaning which it acquires through its application in the natural sciences. In this case, the constituents of the content of a presentation can be called parts of a presentation, only one has to insist that by the presentation one always understands in this context the content of the presentation, never the act of presentation. If one wants to stress this point, one can speak of parts of contents of presentations rather than of parts of presentations or one can speak, whenever the context excludes misinterpretations, of parts of contents.

The constituents of the object of a presentation are to be contrasted with the constituents of the corresponding content; the parts of the object with the parts of the content; they must as little be confused with each other as the content of a presentation with its object. It was

[13] Sigwart, *op. cit.*, vol. 1, para. 41.
[14] Lotze, *Logik* (Leipzig 1881), p. 46.

necessary to draw a sharp distinction between these two kinds of constituents, because the relationship between the parts of a content of a presentation and the parts of the corresponding object can only be investigated with any expectation of success if one pays attention to this difference.

# 9. THE MATERIAL CONSTITUENTS OF THE OBJECT

As mentioned at the end of the last chapter, whenever one speaks of the parts of a complex object, one has to consider, in addition to what one calls a part in the usual sense, also the relations which obtain among these parts and which are no less constituents of the complex whole. The totality of the first mentioned kind of parts is customarily called the *material* [*Stoff*] of which the whole consists, while the totality of the constituents of the second kind is called the *form* [*Form*] of the whole. We distinguish, accordingly, for every complex between its material and its formal constituents.[1]

There are a great many kinds of material constituents of which an object can be composed. These kinds can be classified from various points of view, and such classifications have indeed been attempted in different ways. It is not our task here to investigate what kinds of parts and what kinds of wholes there are. This would be the topic of a systematic theory of relations which would describe and classify the ways in which something can be a part of a whole and in which a whole can consist of parts. We are here only interested in what is common to all kinds of parts and to all forms of composition of parts, that is, in the type to which every synthesis belongs, and which is the basis for the various ways in which a whole can be composed.

For this purpose it is not necessary to know all the elements of which the objects of presentations are composed, in the way in which Sigwart tries to list them.[2] Furthermore, the way in which a complex *originates* from what is simple, the genetic origin of the complex, need not be touched upon here. What we presuppose is that there are complex entities.

The word 'part,' 'constituent,' has to be taken in its widest sense. Not only in what ordinary language or the mathematician calls a part

[1] Compare Erdmann, *op. cit.*, para. 23.
[2] *Op. cit.*, vol. 2, para. 65 ff.

is meant by the word, but generally everything that can be distinguished in or about the object of a presentation, irrespective of whether one can speak of a real analysis into the distinguishable parts or merely of an analysis in thought.

With these presuppositions in mind, one has to distinguish, first of all, between those material parts of a whole which are simple and those which can in turn be analyzed into parts. If the material parts of an object can be analyzed into further parts, then we speak of closer and more distant parts.[3] Whenever it is important to distinguish more precisely between closer and more distant parts, one can distinguish between material parts of first, second, etc., order. Material parts of first order are then those parts into which the object as a whole is divided. The parts of the parts which are obtained from an analysis of the whole object are material parts of second order. Etc. For example, if one analyzes a book into its pages and its cover, then the pages and the cover are material parts of first order of the book. If one now distinguishes between the color and the size of the pages, on the one hand, and the front and the back of the cover, on the other, then these are parts of the second order of the book, but parts of first order of the pages and the cover, respectively.

It is clear that the difference between material parts of the first and the following orders may often be merely relative in still another respect. While in some cases the more distant parts can only be gotten through a division of the closer parts, so that this division has to occur first, in other cases, a single analysis may yield immediately also those constituents which appear as constituents of second order when two analyses are performed. If one analyzes an hour into minutes and these into seconds, then the seconds are constituents of second order of the hour. But instead of dividing an hour into sixty minutes and every minute into sixty seconds, one can divide the hour in one fell swoop, as it were, into three-thousand-six-hundred seconds. If one does, then the seconds appear as constituents of *first* order of the hour.

When one deals with more distant parts which can also appear as closer parts of another division, then one unhesitatingly calls these more distant parts as well parts of the whole; not so if the more distant parts can only be gained after the whole has first been decomposed into its closer parts. In this case, ordinary usage rebels against calling the more distant parts, parts of the whole. Seconds are called no less parts of hours than parts of minutes; but one has scruples about calling the

[3] Compare Bolzano, *op. cit.*, para. 58.

windows of houses parts of a city, even though they are more distant parts of a city; for they can only be gotten after the analysis of the *collectivum* "city" into closer parts has taken place.

However, this is not true without exception. Ordinary usage – influenced by scientific opinion in important points – calls in some cases more distant parts of an object parts of this object, even though these parts are only arrived at after an analysis of the object into its closer parts has occurred. This happens, for example, when we deal with the chemical composition of something out of atoms of the respective elements. Atoms are more distant constituents inasmuch as they can only be gotten through an analysis of molecules, which must be called the closer constituents. Nevertheless, one speaks of atoms as parts of an object, which is then conceived of as being composed of them.

In spite of these exceptions, the relationship between close and more distant constituents of an object seems well suited to serve as a basis for a classification of the possible constituents of objects, a basis which would guarantee the completeness of the classification because of its very nature. The old philosophy touched upon this matter when it distinguished between parts which are and parts which are not homonymous with the whole. This circumstance could be used as a basis for a subdivision; the main division would have the basis mentioned above. Accordingly, one would have to distinguish between simple and complex parts; and the complex parts would have to be divided into those whose constituents can be parts of the same order of the whole as the parts of the whole which are composed of them, etc.

There is still another division of the material constituents of an object. There are material constituents which can enter in only one way into a complex whole. Others, however, can function in different ways as constituents of an object. Red, for example, is a constituent of a red ball in one sense, constituent of the spectrum in another, and constituent of all mixed colors in which it is contained in a third sense. Extension – not in the sense of a definite magnitude, but as extension in one, two, or three dimensions – is, whenever it occurs as a constituent, a constituent of the extended object in one and the same way. The same holds for time inasmuch as it occurs as a constituent of an object, as a "duration" of objects.

One finds still a third division of constituents. According to it, there are constituents which can also exist by themselves, separated from the whole whose parts they are. A second group comprises those constituents whose existence depends on others, while the existence of these other constituents does not depend on them. To a third and final group belong those constituents which depend for their existence mutually on each other.[4] However, we cannot agree with this division of the material parts of objects, because it is based on the supposition that parts *exist*. When we here talk about objects and their constituents, we disregard, according to our agreed upon presuppositions, the real, possible, or impossible existence of objects and their parts and consider the objects only insofar as they are presented through corresponding presentations, that is, only as objects of presentations.

But if this division of constituents concerns their being conceivable and, accordingly, divides constituents into those which can be conceived of independently of each other and those which can only be conceived of as mutually or one-sidedly dependent, then it is not so much a division of parts of objects as of constituents of contents of presentations. And from this point of view we shall have to take another look at it.

[4] Compare Hoefler, *op. cit.*, para. 15.

# 10. THE FORMAL CONSTITUENTS OF THE OBJECT

The formal constituents of an object divide into two groups, depending on whether one considers the relations between the constituents on the one hand, and the object as a whole, on the other, or the relations which obtain among the constituents. We call the relations which obtain between the object and its constituents *primary* formal constituents of the object, while we call the relations holding among the constituents themselves "*secondary* formal constituents."

The definition of primary formal constituents of an object as the relations between the parts and the whole which consists of these parts is, on second glance, ambiguous. For there are two kinds of relations between a whole and its parts. One kind comprises the relations by means of which the parts are parts of this particular whole. For the parts "do not just stand there side by side, they are not just in the whole as in a comprehensive framework; rather, a causal relation exists – the whole *comprehends* the parts, holds them together, *has* them. . . . The enduring relationship between the whole and its parts is an action by the whole on the parts or by the parts on the whole; the whole has, that is, holds the parts, ties them together into a unity by means of an action, the parts "form" the whole."[1]

We call these relationships between the whole and its parts – which, from the viewpoint of the whole, is called the "having" of the parts; from the viewpoint of the parts, the "forming" of the whole – "primary formal constituents in the strict sense."

In addition to these primary formal constituents in the strict sense, a complex object contains also other relations whose terms consist, on the one hand, of its parts, on the other, of the object as a whole. For example, the whole object is larger than its parts taken singly; the object as a whole can be similar to its parts in various respects and dissimilar in other ways; the relationship of coexistence can obtain

[1] Sigwart, *op. cit.*, vol. I, para. 6, 3 a and b.

between a whole object and its parts (if, for example, the object is a thing), or the relationship of succession (if, for example, the object is a motion, a change, or a year, or an hour). All these relations are different from the relationship between the parts as such and the whole as such. We call them "primary formal constituents of the object in an extended sense."

Since the primary formal constituents in the extended sense can be related to the formal constituents in the strict sense – since they may, for example, presuppose the latter, but since they may also obtain when the parts are not conceived of as parts of a whole, but as independent objects – both kinds of primary formal constituents yield terms for new relations. We call these "relations relations of second *degree*," using this term for all relations whose terms are relations. Analogously, one would then call relationships between relations of second degree "relations of third degree," etc.

If the primary material constituents of an object are in turn complex – a supposition fulfilled in the vast majority of all cases – then one can discern in them, insofar as they in turn are considered as objects, all the earlier mentioned primary formal constituents. For the material constituents of second order, too, stand to the material constituents of first order first of all in the relation of being a part of a whole (primary formal constituents in the strict sense); but there exist, furthermore, relations between the just mentioned material constituents which are different from the relation between the whole and its parts as such (primary formal constituents in the extended sense). Thus we have, in analogy to the material constituents of first, second, ... order, primary formal constituents of first, second, ... rank, namely, those in the strict sense as well as those in the extended sense. And since the analysis of an object can rarely be considered finished when it has arrived at the material constituents of second order, there follow after the primary formal constituents of first and second rank those of third and fourth rank.

One may think that these primary formal constituents have to be distinguished as constituents of first, second, ... *order*. But we need this term for a different purpose. Just as we called more distant material constituents those constituents which result from an analysis of the closer material constituents, in a similar fashion more distant formal constituents result from an analysis of the closer formal constituents. Up to now, it has been possible only in rare cases to analyze relations as such. They have usually appeared to be something simple, mocking all attempts at analysis. Think of relations like coexistence, sameness, etc. But whenever analysis is possible, the complex relation does not appear as composed of relations which have the same terms as the complex relation; rather, the analysis of the complex relation involves an analysis of *one* or *both* of its terms. The first is the case for the causal relation. The analysis of the causal relation is bound up with an analysis of one of its terms if it is defined as follows: A totality $U$ of facts $u_1$, $u_2$, ..., $u_n$ is called "the cause of the start $W$ of a process" and $W$ "the effect of $U$," if at the same moment at which the totality $u_1$, $u_2$, ..., $u_n$ is completed, $W$ occurs with necessity.[2] A dependency of $W$ on $u_1$, $u_2$, ..., $u_n$ replaces the causation of $W$ by $U$. The second case occurs whenever the similarity relation can be viewed as a partial identity. We say that $A$ (= a b c d e) is similar to $B$ (= a b c δ ε) and thus assert a relation between $A$ and $B$ which can be reduced to three identity relations with the terms $a$, $b$, and $c$.

The first of these two cases occurs if one analyzes the relation by means of which certain objects are parts of a complex. If these parts are in turn complex, then the relations between the whole and its material constituents of first order reduce to as many relations between the whole and its material constituents of second order as the whole has constituents of the second kind. And we have to call these latter relations "primary formal constituents of second order." We may discover, in a similar fashion, such relations of third, fourth, ... order. And this does not only hold for the primary formal constituents in the strict sense, but also for those in the extended sense.

All the listed relations of different rank and different order can and will stand in new relations (of second, third, ... degree) to each other. And this will be possible in two ways. Either the terms of these relations are relations which belong to the same or to different ranks, or one term of the new relation is a relation of the first, second, ... order, while the other is a relation of the first, second, ... rank. In this fashion, there occur different groups of relations of higher order.

This seems to exhaust what needs to be said in general about the kinds of primary formal constituents and the relations which are possible among them.

As far as these primary formal constituents themselves are concerned, they prove to be of a great variety. For, depending on the kind of material constituent in question, the way in which they "form" the whole and the way in which the whole "has" them will be different.

[2] Hoefler, *op. cit.*, para. 27.

From this point of view, a classification of the primary formal constituents would have to be based on a division of material constituents; but we avoid this on purpose. However, one must keep in mind that primary formal constituents always have the same genus, but that they can be of entirely different kinds; and thus Sigwart has a right to say that it can "only be confusing if, without exception, everything – for example, three-sided figure, dark redness, rotating motion, yellow body, core enveloped by a cover, etc. – is expressed by the same formula $A = a\ b\ c\ d$, as if this juxtaposition were an expression of the same connection in all cases."[3]

But even though different *kinds* of synthesis occur in Sigwart's examples, nevertheless it is in each case, in regard to the *genus*, the same synthesis of parts and whole, a synthesis which remains the same in many different forms. In this sense, every complex object can be viewed as the function of its parts, and the formula used by Lotze and Zimmermann to designate the constituents of the content of a presentation and their relationship to the total content can be applied to complex objects in general. The object is then expressed this way: $O = f(P_1, P_2, P_2, \ldots P_3)$, where the $P_n$ are its parts, namely, the material constituents of first order. Depending on the category of object under study and the kind of material constituents, the way in which the constituents are contained in the whole will be different and, hence, will be designated by $f, f', F, F', \varphi, \varphi'$, etc. For, the sign for the function is the sign for the containment of the parts in the whole, the sign for the fact that the whole "has" the parts, that the parts "form" the whole. If the object can be analyzed into more distant material constituents, that is, if $P_1, P_2, \ldots P_n$ are in turn complex objects, then the first formula must be elucidated by additional formulae of the kind: $o_1 = P_1 = f_1(p_1, p_2, \ldots, p_n)$, $o_2 = P_2 = f_2(\pi_1, \pi_2, \ldots, \pi_n)$, etc.

As important as this primary formal constituent is, namely, the relation between the whole as such and its parts as such, as great are the difficulties which surround its concept. We are faced with these difficulties as soon as we raise questions about the terms of this relation. We have always talked about relations between the whole and its parts. But the whole already contains the part. And to answer that a part stands in relations to all other parts of a whole is a subterfuge which does not help any; for these relations are different from the one which holds between the parts and the whole. This difficulty, already mentioned in the Middle Ages, is not at all solved by our previous con-

[3] Sigwart, *op. cit.*, vol. 1, para. 41, 9.

siderations; to the contrary, these considerations put it in a clearer light.[4] The solution of this difficulty has to be the task of special investigations. For our purposes, it must suffice to mention it for the sake of completeness; what we say about the primary formal constituents holds even if we assume that those difficulties will never find their solutions.

Now if it is a matter of finding a name for the peculiar relation which obtains between a part and a whole inasmuch as the former belongs to the latter and the latter has the former, then I know of no better one than the name '*property*' [*Eigenschaft*]. One may object, at first, against this term that it is synonymous with "condition" [*Beschaffenheit*], and hence that it is only a different name for one of the terms of the relation – the one that is had by, that belongs to the whole – but not a name for this relation of having itself. The answer to this is, however, that the expression 'property,' as it occurs in a certain complex expression, means nothing else but "to belong to," namely, in the expression "body-property" [bondage, *Leibeigenschaft*]; and also that the word is in other cases used as often to designate a relationship as to designate one of its terms. For, one calls the color no less a property of a thing than its being colored, that is, the having of color; and if one lists among the properties of a geometric figure "being equilateral," one obviously means by that the having of equal sides. A reference to ordinary use thus decides neither for nor against our choice; for there are a great number of names which are used to desginate a relation as well as one of its terms. The word 'possession,' for example, sometimes means the act of possessing, hence the relationship between a possessor and something possessed, sometimes, however, it means the something which is possessed; hence the analogy with 'property' is complete, since it, too, designates, according to ordinary use, sometimes the relationship between something that has something and something that is had, but at other times, the something which is had. Similarly for expressions like necessity, impossibility, sequence, and the like. The designation of musical intervals like prime, second, etc. belong here, too, since they sometimes

[4] Abelard: *De divisione et definitione*, p. 471 ed. Cousin. "Fuit autem, memini, magistri nostri Roscellini tam insana sententia, ut nullam rem partibus constare vellet, sed sicut solis vocibus species, ita et partes adscribebat. Si quis autem rem illam, quae domus est, rebus aliis, pariete scilitet et fundamento, constare diceret, tali ipsum argumentatione impugnabat: Si res illa, quae est paries, rei illius, quae domus est, pars est, cum ipsa domus nihil aliud sit, quam ipsa paries et tectum et fundamentum, profecto paries sui ipsius et ceterorum pars erit; at vero quomodo sui ipsius pars fuerit? Amplius, omnis pars naturaliter prior est toto suo; quomodo autem paries prior se et allis dicetur, cum se nullo modo prior sit?" Quoted by Prantl, *op. cit.*, vol. 2, p. 80.

designate the distance between two tones, sometimes, the tone which differs from a given one in a certain way. Expressions which end with 'ation,' like signification, presentation, designation, etc., are perhaps all names, sometimes of relations, sometimes of one of their terms. Further, think of words like 'acquaintance,' 'kinship,' 'nearness,' 'remoteness,' and surely you will admit that ordinary use allows us to use certain words equally for relations and for their terms. Here and there, certain conditions may cause a differentiation between names, so that there is a separate designation for a term, on the one hand, and the relation itself, on the other; such differentiations appear as pairs of expressions like 'color,' 'coloring,' and the like; but the feeling for this differentiation soon disappears and one speaks of the coloring and the color of an object without connecting different meanings with the two expressions.

Ordinary use thus knows two meanings of the word 'property'; one means a relation, the second, one of the terms of this relation. In scientific discourse, whenever the word seems to have a precise meaning, it is used to designate the metaphysical parts of an object,[5] in contrast to the entity to which these parts belong, and one speaks in this sense of things and their properties, contrasting them with each other in a certain way. But this scientific use is not at all fixed; for even in books of the philosophical sciences, we find the word 'property' used for the 'four-corneredness' of a figure, hence as meaning the having of four corners. Since we can therefore assume that the name 'property' is not as yet an established *terminus technicus*, like the expressions 'judgment,' 'consequence,' and 'necessity' (logical and physical), we may perhaps propose that the word be used exclusively for the relationship between a whole as such and each one of its closer and more distant parts as such. The word 'property' could be replaced by expressions like 'metaphysical part,' or 'condition.'

The property in the sense which was customary until now – as a term of the relation between whole and part – was restricted to the area of metaphysical parts. In the exclusive sense here proposed – as the relation itself between part and whole – the expression applies not only to the relation between the whole and its metaphysical parts, but also to the relations between the whole and all its parts, no matter to what

[5] By metaphysical part, one understands what can be distinguished in or about a whole by means of the ability to abstract, but what cannot really be separated from the whole. Extension, color, weight – in short, everything called a property in ordinary discourse – are metaphysical parts of the objects which have these properties.

kind these belong. A regiment or a soldier cannot be called a property of an army, a minute cannot be called a property of an hour; only the color, the extension, the weight, etc. of an object can in this sense be called properties. Not so, if by property one understands the relation itself. In this case, the having of regiments and of soldiers as parts (or, as one says, being composed of regiments and soldiers) are as much properties of the army as consisting of minutes (= having of minutes as parts) is a property of an hour; and this in the very same sense in which the coloring and three-dimensionality (= the having of a color and of three dimensions as metaphysical parts) are, for example, properties of a body.

The designation of the primary formal constituents of an object as 'properties' of it can be justified from still another point of view. These relations between the whole as such and its parts can be discerned in complex objects, but they cannot be separated from them other than *in abstracto*. Hence these relations fall under the "properties" of an object even if the word is taken in its common, popular meaning. This explains the fact that one calls the coloring (= the having of a color), etc. properties of an object. From this viewpoint, the use of the expression which is here proposed as the sole designation of the relation by virtue of which the parts form a whole appears as a limitation of the popular use of the word. And that scientific terminology may introduce such limitations is shown by numerous examples taken from various sciences. One merely has to recall such words as 'acid,' 'mass,' 'function,' etc.

But if the relations of "having" which obtain between a whole and its parts are in turn parts of the whole – and that they are such parts cannot be denied, and justifies us in calling them formal *constituents* of the object – then these relations are had by the object no less than the material constituents. But now there arises an infinite complication in that these second primary formal constituents are likewise had by the whole. Perhaps it is just this infinite nesting of primary formal constituents which contains the key to the answer to the question concerning the nature of the relation which holds the parts together in a whole.

Be that as it may, it is sufficient for our purposes to keep these primary formal constituents in mind; we call them "properties of objects" or, in order to avoid possible misunderstandings arising from the popular meaning of the word, "*property relations*."

The material constituents of an object, however, are not the only ones which are "had" by an object. Disregarding the just mentioned property relations, which hold between a whole and its primary formal constituents, we can also distinguish in a complex object various relations among its parts. These relations are the secondary formal constituents of the object. What distinguishes them from the primary ones is that the object as a whole never occurs among their terms, but only parts of it.

Depending on what these parts are, one has to distinguish:

1. Relationships among the primary formal constituents. These relations are characterized by the fact that all property relations of one and the same object share one term. Another relationship which belongs here is that of the causal dependency which may obtain between one property relation and another of the same object. The having of the property expressed by the Pythagorean theorem by an object depends on the fact that the object called "rectangular triangle" has three straight sides and one right angle. These secondary formal constituents are the most important one for our knowledge of the objects of presentations, and it is the endeavor of every science to discover in the objects of its domain as large a number as possible of such relationships whose terms are property relations. The totality of property relations from which one can derive, because of causal dependency, all other property relations of an object is called the essence [*Wesen*] of the object.[6]

The relations among the primary formal constituents may also belong to the field of relations of comparison in that all the material consti-

[6] Sigwart, *op. cit.*, vol. 1, para. 40, 2. Compare also para. 23, 4 and, further, Hoefler, *op. cit.*, 94 A: "In regard to a thing whose properties we discover gradually and empirically, the more properties we discover of it on which depend all of its other properties and relations to other things, the more shall we be convinced that we have gained a deeper insight into its 'nature.' And the characteristics of our presentation of that thing" (Hoefler thinks of these as constituents of the content of a presentation) "which correspond to the properties of the thing deserve then, before all others, to be called 'essential,' and the concepts formed from them deserve to be called 'natural.' Since the formation of nothing but natural concepts presupposes a complete survey of all properties and relations of objects, some have called the formation of natural concepts, not inappropriately, the ultimate goal of investigation in general." Only, Hoefler understands by the properties of things their conditions; but these cannot stand in that mutual causal dependency which is here demanded. Nothing follows for a plane triangle from its right angle; only because the triangle "*has* a right angle," in addition to other constituents, does there follow the having of the peculiarity expressed by the Pythagorean theorem. And Sigwart obviously means just this when he says (at the last mentioned place): "We think of the *unity* of things as their persisting foundation – not affected by the differences in time – which necessitates this property or activity as constant or as in certain fluctuation." The same thought seems to have occurred to Trendelenburg when he argues against the "accidental view" of Herbart that the derivation of the characteristics of a thing is based on the penetration of *genus* and *differentia* in the thing. This penetration is nothing else but the circumstance that *genus* and *differentia* appear as parts of one and the same uniform thing.

tuents of an object may be had by it either in the same way or in different ways; depending on the kind of material constituents and the kind of composition into a uniform whole which is thus determined, there may appeal quite different secondary formal constituents of second degree.

All of these secondary formal constituents are secondary formal constituents in the strict sense, since they obtain among the primary formal constituents and these latter are based on the distinction between a whole as such and its parts. Of course, they, too, divide into more distant secondary constituents (of second, third, . . . order) if the relations among the primary formal constituents are complex.

2. In addition to relations among its primary formal constituents, every object has relations among its material constituents. These relations are of two kinds. Either their nature depends on the primary formal constituents; then they are relations which belong to parts of the object as such just insofar as they are parts. Or the relations belong to the parts of the object regardless of the fact that they are parts, and they hold as well if the parts which are combined into a whole are conceived of as independent objects. For example, a secondary formal constituent of the first kind is the relative position of the three sides of a triangle. The three sides are material constituents of the triangle; *as such* they have such a relative position that each end point of a side coincides with an end point of another side. The relationship between the lengths of the sides by virtue of which two together are longer than the third is also a relation between the material constituents of the triangle which holds between them insofar as they are parts of the object called "triangle." But this relationship can also hold between the three sides when they are not combined into a triangle; however, it is indeed the condition for this combination. In this respect, it belongs in the middle between the relations which belong to the parts of a whole as such and those relations which hold among the parts even if they are conceived of as independent objects. What belongs completely to this second group of secondary formal constituents is, for example, the relationship of equality among the three sides of a triangle. Relations of the second kind determine the form of the combination of the material constituents into a uniform whole only in a more figurative manner, and we call them therefore "secondary formal constituents in the figurative sense" in distinction to those mentioned first, namely, the secondary formal constituents in the strict sense.

But the secondary formal constituents are not thereby exhausted.

For the relations just mentioned can serve as terms for further relationships. The condition that the three sides of a triangle stand in the relationship $a + b > c$, is a relation between the property relations which unite the sides into a triangle and the secondary formal constituents which hold among the sides.[7] And not only are there relations between primary and secondary formal constituents of an object, but also among the latter alone, like, for example, the relative magnitudes of the angles of a triangle; for the angles are nothing but the expression of the relative positions of the sides of the triangle.

Furthermore, if one realizes that the material constituents of an object can be divided up in turn, then one will be able to discover in each such constituent of first order all the earlier mentioned relationships, since this constituent, conceived of as an object, has the constituents of second order analogically to the manner in which the whole has the constituents of first order, and since also secondary formal constituents occur in a corresponding way. But, at the same time, the material constituents of second order of an object stand in certain relations to those of first order; the more distant parts of an object, too, are had by the whole, though only mediately; the property relations between the whole and its closer parts and the property relations between the property relations and its more distant parts are the terms of a number of relations which hold between them. And the relations between the closer and the more distant property relations are in turn also terms of relations; and relations also hold between the secondary formal relations of first rank (that is, the secondary formal relations which have as terms the material constituents of first order) and the secondary formal relations of second rank.

The number of formal constituents of an object is determined by the number of its material constituents, and where the latter is assignable, where it is not infinitely large, the former must be, up to a certain degree, too. To be sure, this assignability remains almost always a theoretical one, since our earlier considerations show that the variety of constituents which can be discovered through the analysis of an object is tremendous.

[7] The so-called "incompatibility" of marks is based on this; for, two properties or the like can only be called incompatible insofar as they are conceived of as parts of one and the same object.

## 11. THE CONSTITUENTS OF THE CONTENT

The difference between object and content of a presentation is not absolute, but, in Kerry's words, relative.[1] It is true that the content of a presentation cannot at the same time and in the same sense be also the object of this presentation. But nothing prevents the content of a presentation from being conceived of as the object of *another* presentation, and for psychological investigations this is even necessary. This is always the case when one, for example, asserts that one conceives of something. This assertion affirms an object of a presentation, for affirmation and denial, as we have seen, aim at such an object; but the object of affirmation and denial, and hence also of an activity of conceiving which aims at what is affirmed and denied, is the content of a presentation. Therefore, the content of a presentation is always conceived of as the content of that act which aims at the object conceived of through this content; but it can also be presented through a different act, and this in such a way that the content of the earlier act is now the object of the new act of presentation. In regard to the presentation of the horse, the horse is the object of this presentation; in regard to the presentation of the presentation of the horse, however, the presentation of the horse is the object; and it is an object in respect either to its act, or its content, or both, so that the content of the presentation of the horse is an object of the presentation of the presentation of the horse. The content of a presentation can thus quite easily be an object of a presentation if this presentation is a so-called presentation-presentation [*Vorstellungsvorstellung*], that is, the presentation of a presentation.[2]

Since we have dealt with the material and formal constituents of objects regardless of their special nature, what we have said in the

[1] Kerry, *op. cit.*, vol. II, pp. 272 ff. Compare also Ueberweg, *op. cit.*, para. 49.

[2] This expression is due to Bolzano who calls such presentations also "symbolic," a designation which must not be confused with the "symbolic" thinking of Leibniz. (Bolzano, *op. cit.*, para. 90.)

preceding two chapters holds for every kind of object and, hence, also for the contents of presentations, since they, too, can be conceived of as objects. Nothing needs to be added to what we have said there.

But in this connection we must recall the division of the parts of those objects which are not contents of presentations, the one which divides these parts according to whether or not they are conceivable independently of each other (see above p. 49). We cannot apply this division to objects of presentations in general, since it presupposes the existence of the objects and their parts, while our considerations were supposed to apply to all objects, those that exist as well as those that do not. Now, if the contents of presentations are considered to the extent that they can be presented just like anything else, that is, as objects of presentation-presentations, then what we have said about all objects holds for them as well and the division under discussion does not hold generally because it depends on the presupposition of existence. But since we shall speak from now on about the relationship between the object of a presentation, *when it is presented*, and the content of that presentation *through* which it is presented, we shall be dealing with *existing* contents of presentations. For, it is clear that the content of a presentation exists irrespective of whether one is presented with an existing or a nonexisting object. Thus the division under discussion may be of excellent service for the time being. According to this division, the material constituents of the content of a presentation are grouped according to the following three criteria:

1. Parts with mutual separability. These are parts "each of which can be conceived of without conceiving of the others."

2. Parts with mutual inseparability. These are parts "which we cannot conceive of without the others, but which we can distinguish from them."

3. Parts with one-sided separability. "These are parts, for example, *A* and *B*, such that *A* can be conceived of without *B*, but *B* cannot be conceived of without *A*."[3]

Mutually separable parts of the content of a presentation are, for example, the presentations of the individual pages and of the cover of a book inasmuch as they are united in the presentation of the book. For,

[3] This is Hoefler's version (*op. cit.*, p. 51) of the division of the parts of presentations. The expressions 'one-sided separability,' 'mutual separability,' and 'mutual inseparability,' are Brentano's (compare *Vom Ursprung sittlicher Erkenntnis* (Leipzig, 1889), footnote 22, number 2); K. Stumpf calls the separable parts of a content "independent contents," the inseparable ones, "partial contents." (Compare his *Vom psychologischen Ursprung der Raumvorstellungen* (Leipzig, 1873), para. 5.)

one can conceive of the individual pages independently of each other, that is, without the other pages, and also without conceiving of the cover of the book. The same holds for the cover. The presentation of the cover is not dependent in any way on the presentations of the individual pages.

As a typical example of the content of a presentation which consists of mutually inseparable parts, one usually mentions the presentation of something extended and colored. One cannot conceive of a color without conceiving of extension, and conversely.

The presentation of a genus stands to the presentations of its subordinated species in the relationship of one-sided separability. For, the presentation of each species contains the presentation of the genus in such a way that the former is impossible without the latter. One cannot conceive of red, for example, unless this presentation contains the presentation of color. But, conversely, the presentation of color is not necessarily connected with the presentation of red.

This classification of the material constituents of the content of a presentation is based on its formal constituents, on the relations which hold among the material constituents as such, insofar as they are combined into a whole. And this is not an accidental feature, but necessary if one wants to classify objects as parts of a whole. For, they only become parts because they stand in property relations to a whole and, hence, in certain relations to each other; the latter are just the secondary formal constituents of the complex.

The following fact shows that the classification in question only holds on the condition that the contents so classified are conceived of as contents and, hence, exist; and that it does not hold for contents if they are thought of as objects of presentation-presentations. The characterization of each of the three groups of parts of a content speaks of the way in which they can be conceived of or presented; either the being conceived of individual parts depends on the being conceived of other parts, or it does not. But 'being presented' is an ambiguous expression, as we have seen earlier (chapter 4); it designates the being presented as *content* as well as the being presented as *object*. That something is presented as a content means that there is the content of a presentation. And it is true, then, that the content which is meant by the word 'red' does not exist, unless there exists at the same time the content which is meant by the word 'extension,' and conversely. Red cannot be conceived of *in* a presentation (as content), unless *in* the same presentation extension (as content) is also conceived of, and conversely. Things are different if one speaks of being presented in the sense in which we say that an object is presented *through* a presentation. As an object, red can very well be presented *through* a presentation, while *through* that same presentation extension is not presented simultaneously, and conversely. Every time we conceive of a color as such *through* a presentation and make a judgment about it *as* a color, every time we conceive of extension as such *through* a presentation and make a judgment about it *as* extension, we *abstract*; in the first case, from the extension, in the second, from the color. Thus we are quite able to conceive, in an *abstract* way, of what, as a content of a presentation, is dependent on the content of another presentation, so that it cannot be conceived of, that is, exist, separately as a content of a presentation. Hence, the criteria which separate the three groups of parts are sound if we consider what is conceived of in the sense of the content; but they are no longer sound if we understand by 'being conceived of' the being conceived of *through* a presentation, that is, an object.

The kind of composition of the content of a presentation which we have here described, and which agrees with the kind of composition of objects of presentations (to which contents belong as a special class), makes it possible to reintroduce an expression which has been vigorously rejected by modern psychology whenever it was applied to the constituents of the contents of presentations. I have in mind the so-called "co-ordination" of the constituents of the content of a presentation. In what sense certain constituents of a content can be said to be coordinated to each other will be explained below.

It may be mentioned that we shall, in what follows, designate as presentations also those material constituents of contents which cannot occur by themselves as contents. This terminology is not precise; taking the facts into account, one should here really speak of parts of contents. But if one wants to make certain distinctions among the parts of a content with an eye on the parts of the object which are presented through them, then an extremely cumbersome terminology results. This can be avoided if one says, for example: in the presentation of the triangle there are contained the presentations of the sides and of the plane. To be sure, it would be more precise to say: the presentation of the triangle contains material parts of a content through which the three sides and the plane are presented.

## 12. THE RELATIONSHIP BETWEEN THE OBJECT AND THE CONTENT OF A PRESENTATION

Having described the parts of objects and contents, the question now arises as to what relationship there is between the content and the object of one and the same presentation.

A primitive psychology replied readily that the presentation (in the sense of the content) is simply a mental picture of the object and assumed that the question was thereby answered. Now, surely, there must be a relation between the content and the object by virtue of which an object belongs to this particular content, and a content is the content which corresponds to one particular, and no other, object. However, whether it is to be assumed that there is a kind of photographic resemblance between content and object is a question which receives nowadays generally a negative answer.

People have become convinced that the relationship between the presentation and its object is an irreducible, primary relationship which can as little be described as, say, the relationship of incompatibility between two judgments. Kerry emphasizes that the relation between a concept and its objects is fundamental and irreducible. He says that what there is in or about the relation between concept and object that *cannot* be reduced to similarity and equality is just its characteristic feature, namely, the feature of a special belonging of the object to the concept.[1] Now, while Kerry admits that there are other relations between content and object, in addition to this irreducible relation, namely, relations of similarity and equality, other philosophers seem to be inclined to admit only that there is this one relationship between object and content, the relation which consists in the belonging of both the object and the content to one and the same mental act, and they are inclined to deny all other relations between contents and objects. Zimmermann, for example, says that the nature of a content of a concept has no more to do with the nature of its object

[1] Kerry, *op. cit.*, vol. 10, p. 460.

than merely that the latter is an object of the concept and is conceived of through the former.[2]

The question whether there is a further relation, in addition to the one of "being presented through a content," between the object of a presentation and the content which belongs to it, seems to have an affirmative answer in some cases, a negative answer in others. The former seems to hold for contents through which simple objects are presented or, at least, objects are presented *as* simple; the latter seems to hold when complex objects are presented or objects are presented as complex.

That many objects are presented as simple, even when they are in truth not simple, seems indubitable, and such is the case when the parts of an object are not distinguished and it appears as simple. If one steps from a dark room out into the sunlight, then one has a sensory presentation [*Empfindungsvorstellung*] of the light. The object of this presentation is the light, and whoever has this presentation most likely does not analyze its object, at least not for a moment, so that he does not distinguish between its intensity, its color, etc. So long as this analysis does not take place, the object appears as simple and it appears as standing in no other relationship to the content of the presentation than that it is presented through this content. Other relationships can decidedly not be discovered. But as soon as there occurs an analysis of the object into its parts, and it is noticed that just as the object has certain parts, so the content of a presentation can be analyzed into constituents which correspond to the parts of the object, there appears immediately a new relationship between content and object. This relationship consists in this, namely, that the parts of the object are presented through constituents of the content in a way which is determined by the manner in which the parts of the object are united into a whole, uniform object. Hence there is an analogy between the composition of the parts of the object and the composition of the constituents of the content, an analogy, to be sure, of a rather peculiar nature, one which is determined by the relationship of being presented between an object and a content.

To the material constituents of the object of a presentation there correspond first of all certain material constituents of the content. But not all material constituents of the content have as their objects material constituents of the object of the presentation. If, through a presentation of a horse, one is presented with the parts of the horse,

[2] Zimmermann, *op. cit.*, para. 26.

then one is also presented with certain relations among these parts, hence with formal constituents of the object. The material parts of the content thus intend partially material constituents of the corresponding object, partially formal constituents. The totality of the property relations, which unite into a uniform object the individual material constituents, as far as they are distinguished, by virtue of their having one common term, is never missing from these formal constituents. In other words, one is presented with the material parts of an object, not as so many relatively more simple objects, but as parts of a complicated uniform object. But one is also presented with certain relations which obtain among the material constituents of the object, so, for example, with their mutual positions, their mutual casual dependency, or their relative magnitudes, etc. In short, the material as well as the formal constituents of the object of presentation are correlated to material constituents of its content.

As regards the formal constituents of a complex content, those relations seem to be of primary importance by means of which the individual material constituents of the content form parts of a uniform whole, that is, the property relations between the total content and its material parts. The presentations of the color, shape, size, etc. of a sphere stand to the presentation of the sphere in a relationship which is analogical to the relationship between the color, shape, size, etc. of the sphere to the sphere itself. In the same way, the presentations of the color, shape, size, etc. of a sphere stand in relations to each other whose nature is determined by the kind of relations which obtain among the just mentioned metaphysical parts of an object. Ueberweg expresses this by saying that the real relationship of the characteristics of an object must be reflected in the relationship which the parts of the presentation have to each other and to the total presentation. Accordingly, he defines the content of a presentation as the "totality of parts of a presentation standing in the kind of mutual connection which is determined by the corresponding real relationships."[3] These presentations of the relationships between the material constituents of an object determine the arrangement and the mutual relationships of those material constituents of the content through which those material constituents of the object are presented. The relationships which occur among the material constituents of the content because of the presentations of the formal constituents of an object form, in thier totality, what one commonly calls, in regard to the content of a presen-

[3] Ueberweg, *op, cit.*, para. 49.

tation, the "form of synthesis." This form of synthesis is therefore not the totality of the presentations of relations which hol among the material constituents of the content—this is how Hoefler thinks of the matter[4] – but is the totality of these relations themselves. In the definition of the content of a presentation the material as well as the formal constituents must be considered, and it will not do to define the content of a presentation solely as the totality of the characteristics if one, like Hoefler, understands by that presentations, hence, material constituents of the content.

What was said here about the composition of the content of a presentation as compared to the object of a presentation must stand up when we consider concrete examples. The type which we here described can only be justified if it is applicable to every single case. We shall therefore attempt now to give some examples. There are two circumstances which tend to make this attempt more difficult and which may make its realization appear less successful. First of all, there is the difficulty of listing those constituents of the object or of the content of a presentation which are of the same order, hence co-ordinated with each other as parts. There is great danger that one puts close and more distant constituents side by side, instead of deriving them from each other through successive divisions. If one makes this mistake, then it is easily possible that there occur deviations from the type we have described which put this type in doubt. A second difficulty consists in the often lamented fact that the ultimate, simple constituents of presentations, their elements in the truest sense of the term, have not as yet been found. Analysis has not progressed equally far everywhere, so that one may reach a point in the analysis of a simple content of a presentation where a further analysis cannot be carried out for some constituents, while other constituents, of the same order, may well be capable of further analysis.

These two circumstances are liable to prevent a pure occurrence of the type of composition we have described. However, it seems justified to attribute the fault for this imperfection to the type itself at least to no greater degree than to the rather insufficient psychological analysis of contents and to the rather insufficient metaphysical analysis of objects which prevail today. Moreover, these difficulties will be avoided as far as possible by a selection of proper examples.

The situation is very clear for those objects and their presentations which constitute the field of mathematics. We take our first example

[4] Hoefler, *op. cit.*, para. 16.

from this field and analyze the arithmetic series 1, 2, 3, and the corresponding presentation.

The object of the presentation is complex. Its material constituents of first order are the numbers 1, 2, 3. These numbers stand in property relations to the series as a whole. The number 1, the number 2, the number 3, are had by the series as parts and are called, accordingly, "terms of the series." These property relations are the primary formal constituents of first rank in the strict sense. In addition to these, however, there exist also primary formal constituents in the extended sense, since every material constituent of the series is composed of fewer units than the series taken as a whole. That these are primary formal relations in the extended sense follows from the fact that the just mentioned relationship, according to which the series as a whole consists of more units than each one of its terms, also obtains between the series and the numbers 1, 2, 3 if the latter are compared with the series, *not* as terms of the series, but as numbers by themselves. Relations of second degree hold between the primary formal constituents in the strict sense and those in the extended sense; the latter, for example, are conditions for the former, since no series can consist of terms which, taken individually, would be greater than the series considered as a whole.

The secondary formal constituents of the object called "series" have as terms, first of all, the primary formal constituents in the strict sense. All property relations between the series and the numbers which form it are of the same kind; the first term stands to the whole series in the same relationship of being had as the second term, and the second term, in the same as the third. The kind of combination into a whole is the same for all parts. There are also relations among the primary formal constituents in the extended sense. If every number of the series is smaller than the series taken together, then there exists, among these relations between the terms and the series, also the relationship of homogeneity. Secondary formal constituents occur among the material constituents of first order. The most important constituent of this kind is the so-called law of the series which shows in what relationship the first term stands to the second, and the second to the third. But here, too, one must distinguish between the secondary formal constituents in the strict sense, to which those just mentioned belong, and those in the extended sense. For, that 2 is greater than 1 and 3 is greater than 2, is a relationship among the three numbers which holds for them, even if they are not united as terms of a series; hence these are secondary formal constituents in the extended sense. And there are relations of second degree among these last mentioned formal constituents, since the difference in magnitude is the same for all three material constituents of first order; it is always the unit.

Further formal constituents in the strict sense can be pointed out for the series; they determine the arrangement of the terms in the series and consist in that 1 is the first, 3 the last, and 2 is the middle term of the series.

Whether the primary formal constituents in the strict sense divide into constituents of second order remains an open question as long as the nature of the property relation between a whole and its parts has not been classified. Should this relation turn out to be complex, then a further analysis would yield primary formal constituents in the strict sense which would be of second order.

If the relations by virtue of which a number is greater than another can be reduced to a relation of equality and relation of difference, then these latter relations are secondary formal constituents of second order. But these relations presuppose that the material constituents of first order are themselves analyzable. And this is the case for the second term and the third term of the series, while the first term seems to have no material constituents of second order. The material constituents of second order are the units of which the numbers 2 and 3 consist. They are "had" by the corresponding material constituents of first order; hence there are as many property relations between a material constituent of first order and the respective material constituents of second order as there are of the latter contained in the former. To the material constituents of second order there correspond formal constituents of second rank, those in the extended sense as well as those in the strict sense. To the former kind belongs the equality between all material constituents of second order, since these are all the unit; to the latter kind belongs the law of additive connection according to which numbers which – in a positive or negative sense – are greater than the unit originate from the unit.

But this does not as yet exhaust the variety of parts of the object called "arithmetic series." The analysis has still to be completed in two directions. For, there obtain also relations among the material constituents of different order, relations which are not exhausted by the property relations, even though these, too, have as their terms material constituents of different order. Such a relation, for example, is the relation of equality or inequality which obtains between the material constituents of first order, the terms of the series, and the material constituents of second order, the units.

If one pursues the analysis in a second direction, then it yields a series of material constituents of different orders. When we analyzed the series into the terms of which it consists, we took into account only *one* kind of material constituent. In addition to this kind, the series also has material constituents which belong to that genus of parts which is called a metaphysical part. Such material constituents are, in this case, the finiteness of the series, the relationships in which it stands to other series, and so on. Since each of these constituents allows for a further analysis, there occur, in addition to those already mentioned, numerous more distant material and formal constituents of first order, second order, etc.

From this point of view, one can even discern constituents for these material constituents of first order which appeared to be simple. For, even though the number 1 – fractions of the unit aside – cannot be further analyzed into numbers, we can nevertheless discern relations in which this unit stands to other numbers. These relations must be counted among the constituents of the object to which they are attached because they are affirmed or rejected, together with the object, in a judgment about the object. They are also designated by the name for the object, although only in that same implicit way in which they are judged through a judgment which is about the object. It follows that there are no simple objects of presentations in the strict sense of this word. This assertion does not contradict the assumption according to which one distinguished between simple and complex *things*. For, here one abstracts once and for all from the relations in which the thing stands to other objects. And with this presupposition one is surely justified in talking of simple things.

In regard to the composition of the content of the presentation which has as its object the finite arithmetic series under consideration, it is first of all clear that not *all* constituents of the object are presented through the corresponding presentation. After Bolzano's exhaustive studies there can no longer be any doubt about this.[5] Furthermore, since one and the same object can be presented through different presentations, several presentations would have to be investigated as regards the relationship between their contents and the object. Now we shall

[5] Bolzano, *op. cit.*, para. 64.2. By the way, this follows from the fact just mentioned that the relations between an object and others must also be counted among its constituents. Since their number is then boundless, it is immediately clear that not *all* the constituents of an object can be presented through a (intuitive) [*anschauliche*] presentation of it.

assume that the series is presented in intuition [*anschaulich*]; that is, presented neither symbolically in Leibniz's sense, nor through an indirect presentation of another kind.[6]

The content of the presentation of the arithmetic series under consideration consists, first of all, of material constituents of first order. These are the relatively more simple presentations of the numbers which form the series, of the property relations between the terms of the series, on the one hand, and the series itself, on the other, as well as of the secondary formal constituents of the series, of the law according to which the series is formed. And this holds for all presentations of a complex object which is not conceived of as simple.

Each content of such a presentation contains three groups of material constituents of first order. The first group is formed by the presentations of the material constituents of first order of the object; the second group comprises the presentations of the property relations which obtain between the object as a unified whole and its material constituents of first order; the third group consists of the presentations of the secondary formal constituents of the object.

Among all these material first-order constituents of the content there obtain relations, that is, formal constituents of the content of first degree. The terms of these relations belong in pairs partly to the same group, partly to different groups of the material constituents. For not only do the presentations of the terms of the series stand to each other in certain relations, but relations obtain also between every presentation of a term of the series and the presentation of the corresponding property relation, as well as among the presentations of the property relations, and finally between these presentations and the presentations of the formal constituents of first order of the series. It may be the ease that the nature of the relations can be described only very rarely.

It appears to be the case that the material constituents of first order are also the last ones which are presented through a presentation as distinct from each other. There is a peculiar fact concerning the material constituents of second and all possible further orders. These are indeed presentations through the content; for, if this were not the case, no material constituent of first order could be presented, since it consists of those of second order. But since the fact that the terms of the series consist of units is not *noticed*, because of the limitations of

[6] On the concept of the intuitive and the nonintuitive as well as the indirect presentation, see *Marty*, *Vierteljahrsschrift fuer wissenschaftliche Philosophie*, vol. 14, p. 67, footnote; and Hoefler, *op. cit.*, para. 15, IV; and para. 26.

consciousness, the presentations of these terms appear as something which is in fact *undivided*, though divisible. The same holds, for example, for every presentation of a continuum. If one conceives of a line, then one must obviously also conceive of all of its points. Now, one does conceive of the points, but without noticing it, and the presentation of the line therefore gives the impression of being simple.[7]

In view of this peculiar fact, it may appear questionable whether the analysis of the content of the presentation of a series should be continued or not. But since such an analysis of the material constituents of first order of the content into those of second order would result in relationships which are analogous to the ones that result from an analysis of the total content into constituents of first order, the analysis which we have so far outlined in order to give an example may suffice.

The situation is not so clear for presentations of objects, and for objects themselves if they belong to the category of "things." A square piece of white paper lying in front of me on the table may serve as an example.

The material constituents of first order of this sheet of paper are the materials of which it is made, its position, and its duration. As material constituents of second order have to be mentioned: in regard to the material, its color, weight, and extension; in regard to the position, the individual spatial relations to me, to the table, and to other things; in regard to the duration, its beginning and its end. In regard to the color, one has to distinguish (as material constituents of third order of the object) between its hue, its lightness, and its saturation; in regard to the extension, between the three dimensions and its boundaries; in regard to the beginning and the end of the duration, the relations which obtain between the beginning and end of this duration and other points of time.

For each of the just mentioned constituents of third order, one can also discern constituents of fourth order; if no others, than at least the relations between each material constituent of third order and other objects. But this would lead us too far.

This classification of the material constituents of the object under consideration could be criticized, because constituents seem to be distributed among different orders, when they in reality belong to one and the same order. For example, three-dimensionality and color should not be listed as constituents of the extension and the material, re-

[7] One can speak of an implicit presentation here in a similar sense to an implicit judging. One could say, then, that the more distant constituents of an object, from a certain order on, are only implicitly presentations.

spectively, but rather as constituents of first order of the object, together with position and duration. That this was not done is due to the following consideration. Whatever it is that is had by some object, we call a constituent of the object. But an object has not only its close but also its more distant constituents. The latter are distinguished from the former in that they stand in property relations not only to the total object but also to closer constituents of it, that they are had by them. And this is also the case for three-dimensionality and color. To be sure, the object as a whole has also three dimensions and color, but the former are also had by the extension, the latter, by the material. And this compels us to call the three dimensions and the color more distant constituents of the total object and to assign them to the extension and the material as their close constituents. This relationship must not be confused with the one between the position of the sheet of paper and the sheet of paper as a whole. It is true that the material and its boundary have a position, too, but this is *a different one* from the position of the total object; and the positions of the sheet, of the material and of its boundary are constituents which exhibit a common feature and a certain dependency on each other – but these are secondary formal constituents of the object.

We must not be surprised that the analysis of the object which we call a white sheet of paper has this somewhat odd result. Practical needs do not require that we consider the constituents of an object from the point of view of their mutual arrangement. Rather, what is important in practice are those constituents which are especially suited to distinguish different objects from each other or to compare them with each other in regard to this similarity. And these do not always have to be the closest constituents of an object: the latter are often least suitable for the purpose just mentioned.

The material constituents of first order mentioned above are all had by the object, they stand in property relations to it, in primary formal constituents in the strict sense. Insofar as the constituents of first order are in turn complex, they, too, have property relations. Relations of second degree obtain among these property relations of different ranks. One of these, the one by virtue of which the having on the side of the whole is simultaneously a having on the side of a constituent, we have already mentioned. But there are also relations of second degree among the property relations of the same rank. These belong to the secondary formal constituents of the objects, just like the relationships among the material constituents. Such a relationship obtains, for example, between extension and color; the latter presupposes the former, just as the boundary presupposes three dimensions. Formal constituents in the extended sense are also involved, as, for example, between the saturation of the color of the paper and its position. For, this particular saturation belongs to the color of the paper regardless of the fact that the paper has this particular position.

How large the number of all of the formal constituents of the observed object is can be gauged from what we have said already. To list them all appears to be an unrealistic demand. For our purpose, which consists in the testing of the earlier described type of composition by means of concrete examples, it suffices to show that a "thing," too, can be analyzed into closer and more distant material constituents which are bound together into a unit through primary formal constituents in the strict sense. The remaining formal constituents appear as a necessary consequence of this fact.

The content of the presentation of the white sheet of paper shows a smaller number of constituents than the object. For, the duration of an object is, as a rule, not presented; color, extension, position, and boundedness, as well as the material, are normally the only material constituents among those listed which are presented. The presentation of the color contains the presentation of its constituents only implicitly, while the presentation of boundedness, on the other hand, divides into the presentations of the four sides and of the primary and secondary formal constituents which tie them together. It is easy to see that the three groups of material constituents which we distinguished for the presentation of the series can nevertheless also be found here. It follows, furthermore, that the formal constituents which we attribute to objects are also present in the content of the presentation of the sheet of paper; this follows immediately from the fact that the content of every presentation is an object (of another presentation).

The sheet of paper served as an example of a presentation whose object belongs to the category of "thing." Earlier, we considered the composition of an object and of a presentation of it which was a collection [*collectivum*]. But the type of composition of contents and objects which we described above occurs also for the category of property in the ordinary sense, as occasional hints have shown. We were able to refer to an analysis of color into the metaphysical constituents of hue, lightness, and saturation. All these material constituents are had by a "color," hence stand to it in property relations, while they stand to each other in relations which are secondary formal constituents of first rank. It is not necessary to show in detail that the content of the presentation of a color is composed according to the same principles which we found in connection with our previous examples.

But what we have said does not only apply to properties in the ordinary sense, it also holds for all other objects and their ideas; and that no less for a tone than for a motion, for brevity, and for suicide. For example, for motion, we would have to name as material constituents of first order spatial extension and temporal duration; as material constituents of second order we must count: for the spatial extension, the individual places of the space traversed; for time, the individual moments of time. The particular relation between each place and each moment, by means of which the moving body is located for each moment at a place, is a formal constituent of second rank of the motion; the velocity, as a relationship between these formal constituents, a formal constituent of second degree, etc. In short, the assertion seems to be completely justified that the type described earlier holds for all objects as well as for the contents of the respective presentations.

In saying that constituents of objects are coordinated to corresponding parts of contents, we have touched on a point which Lotze, among others, has discussed.[8] This philosopher objects strongly to "the asserted coordination of the characteristics in the content of a concept," whereby he means the arrangement of the material constituents of the content of a presentation within the content. According to Lotze, if it is possible at all to speak in certain cases of such a coordination, then it means nothing more than that all constituents "are equally indispensable for the whole, but that there is in addition *no* order which is somehow articulated." Especially the second part of this view may justifiedly be doubted. For, if what we have said so far is correct, then the content of a presentation is indeed articulated according to a certain law. But one can also talk about a coordination of the constituents of an object and the constituents of a content. By distinguishing between several orders of material and formal constituents, we have also called attention to the difficulty which stands in the way of knowing those constituents which belong to one and the same order. This difficulty did not prevent us from asserting the existence of such constituents. These constituents are then certainly coordinated to each other in the sense that they all stand in the same relationship to the more distant constituents, which can be derived from them, since they

[8] Lotze, *op. cit.*, p. 46 f.

are the "wholes" which are formed from these constituents. Inasmuch as the parts of *one* order are had by the same common whole, they are coordinated with each other. In this sense, one can surely speak of a coordination. And we can even name a characteristic which serves to distinguish between the coordinated parts of a whole and its uncoordinated parts. It consists in the fact that those constituents prove to be coordinated of which one constituent cannot function as the common term of a series of property relations between it and other constituents. This criterion, however, needs a qualification; for it is also fulfilled for parts which are uncoordinated as long as they do not belong to adjacent orders. Hence, the criterion mentioned can only distinguish between coordinated parts and those uncoordinated parts which belong to adjacent orders. But it is just this distinction for which a criterion is desirable, since there is little danger that constituents which belong to distant orders are thought to be coordinated to each other.

To speak of a coordination of constituents in a sense other than the one mentioned above will only do in few cases. But then it is possible. For, constituents of the same order can be coordinated to each other, not only because they are had by a common whole, but also because they are had by it *in the same way*. We pointed out that the kind of property relation depends on the nature of the part as well as on the kind of relations obtaining among the parts, that is, on the secondary formal constituents of the whole. Now, whenever, firstly, all material constituents are of the same order and, secondly, the relations among them (as long as they are formal constituents in the strict sense) are of the same kind, then the parts of the object as well as the parts of the corresponding content can be said to be coordinated in this sense. Obviously, the terms of a series and the like belong here. Hence, when Lotze denies the possibility of any coordination among the parts of the content of a presentation, he goes too far.

We can sum up perspicuously the relations which we have discovered between the content and the object of a perceptual presentation in the following sentences:

1. In regard to contents of presentations whose objects are conceived of as simple, no other relation can be established between content and object than the one which consists in this, namely, that the object of the presentation is presented through its content by virtue of the fact that both, the content and the object belong to the same act of presentation.

2. In regard to complex contents, the constituents of a content

divide into three groups which correspond to material, primary formal, and secondary formal constituents of the object, respectively.

3. The nature of the formal constituents of a content is determined by the characteristics of the formal constituents of the object. This is a special case of the law that the nature of the formal constituents depends on the nature of the material constituents, since the presentations of the formal constituents of an object are material constituents of the content.

# 13. THE CHARACTERISTIC

In addition to the question about the nature of the relationship between the composition of the object of a presentation and the composition of its content, another question arises, namely, the question whether all parts of an object have their equivalent in the content of the presentation which intends it and, conversely, whether all parts of the content of a presentation have corresponding parts in the object. This question about the relationship between the parts of the content and the parts of the corresponding object – investigated by Bolzano, among others – must not be confused with another question which is like it and which is discussed by Kerry in the work we have frequently mentioned. Whereas Bolzano formulates the question as we have done here, Kerry inquires into the differences between the presentation of an object and the presentation of the content which intends this object. We deal then with a comparison between two contents, one of which has as its object the object of a presentation, the other of which has as its object the content of the presentation which intends this object. In concrete terms, Kerry thus compares the content of the presentation of the tree with the content of the presentation of the presentation of the tree.

In regard to the first of these two questions, we have already seen that it has to be answered negatively. Every object has material and formal constituents which are not presented through the corresponding presentation; hence it has constituents to which there correspond no constituents in the content of the presentation. To these constituents which are not presented belong, for example, most of the relations which obtain between an object and other objects and whose number is almost infinite. Furthermore, if the object is an infinite series and, hence, has more than a certain number of constituents, not counting its relations to other objects, then one is presented with only a fraction of these constituents. On closer examination, there may turn out to be no object at all whose presentation contains even the presentations of all the material constituents of the object which are not relations to other objects; no adequate presentation exists of any object.

Therefore, the constituents of every object of a presentation divide into two groups; one group comprises the constituents which are presented through corresponding material constituents of the corresponding presentation; the second group comprises the rest of the constituents of the object. Those constituents of an object which stand to a presentation in a closer relation, so to speak, because they are presented through the presentation of the object, should be called by a special name. The word 'characteristic' can be used for this purpose.

We have tried to show earlier (chapter 8) that this expression should only be used, strictly speaking, to designate parts of objects and never to designate parts of contents if one wants to avoid confusion; we saw how even those philosophers who, in theory, take a characteristic to be a constituent of the content of a presentation become inconsistent and designate by this expression, in the course of their exposition, constituents of the object. Now, if we restrict the applicability of this term even further and use it exclusively as a name for those constituents of the object of a presentation which are presented through the corresponding presentation – constituents which are presented in the content through constituents of the content which correspond to them – then we can invoke important authorities and claim to act in accordance with their intentions. Kant, for example, defines: "A characteristic is that about a thing which constitutes a part of the knowledge of it; or, what is the same, a partial presentation insofar as it is viewed as the basis of knowledge for the whole presentation. ... All thinking is nothing else but conceiving through characteristics. ... All characteristics, viewed as the basis for knowledge, have a twofold use, either an inner or an outer use. The inner use consists in derivation, in order to know the thing itself through the characteristics as the basis for its being known. The outer use consists in comparison, insofar as we can through characteristics compare one thing with others, according to the rules of identity and diversity."[1] If one keeps in mind that Kant means by "knowledge" also presentations, then one cannot mistake the agreement between our definition of the characteristic and Kant's.[2] To be sure, Kant called a characteristic also a "partial presentation," not paying attention to the difference between content

[1] Kant, *Logik*, ed. by Jaesche, Intro. VIII.
[2] *Ibid.*

and object. But this could only happen because Kant – abbreviating the expression too much – called a characteristic "that about a thing which constitutes a part of the knowledge of it." Expressed precisely, the definition should read: a characteristic is that about a thing *whose knowledge* (in the Kantian sense = presentation) constitutes a part of the knowledge (= presentation) of this thing. For, something which is "something about a thing," and which, hence, is part of a thing, cannot seriously be called a partial presentation, that is, a part of a presentation.

Among the most recent philosophers, Trendelenburg – in addition to Kant – seems to conceive of a characteristic in the sense which we have here given to the word. This scholar says that where he speaks of a characteristic, he does not take this word with the subjective meaning which it primarily expresses, so that it would be merely a sign for recognition, but that he takes it in the objective meaning – a meaning which ordinary usage has long associated with it – as that which *forms the concept in the thing.*[3] Although the sense of this definition of the characteristic appears to be somewhat unclear, that interpretation of Trendelenburg's remark seems to reflect his view correctly, according to which one has to understand by the characteristic that "in the thing" which yields the material which is necessary for the forming of a concept of this thing. What corresponds to the concept in the thing are the characteristics of it. If this interpretation is correct, then we can also cite Trendelenburg in regard to the definition of the characteristic here advocated.

Furthermore, Stoeckl's definition of the characteristic seems to belong here. It reads: "One understands by characteristic in general all those features whereby an object is known as what it is and is distinguished from all other objects."[4] These "features" are obviously parts of the object; they must be presented, so that through them an object is known as what it is and is distinguished from all other objects; hence, characteristics are those parts of an object which are presented. Only, Stoeckl's definition seems to be somewhat narrower, since of all the parts of an object which are presented through a presentation only those are called characteristics through which the object "is known as what it is and is distinguished from all others." Hence, what Trendelenburg calls the "subjective meaning" of the word 'characteristic' plays perhaps a greater role here.

[3] Trendelenburg, *Logische Untersuchungen* (Leipzig, 1870), vol. 2, p. 255.
[4] Dr. Alb. Stoeckl, *Lehrbuch der Philosophie*, vol. 1, para. 75.

We may also claim Erdmann's definition of characteristics as a confirmation of ours. He defines: "Characteristics are the distinguishable determinations of the objects of thought; it does not matter whether they are properties, relations of magnitude, or relations of purpose." That by "determinations" one has to understand constituents of the object is shown by a remark in which Erdmann talks about the relationship between the characteristics of an object and the predicates which can be ascribed to this object. "Every characteristic," one reads here, "of an object can be ascribed to it, predicated of it. However, not every predicate of an object is a characteristic. Rather, countless propositions about every object of perception as well as of consciousness are possible which do not mention *constituents* of it, but rather mention relations into which the object, with all its characteristics, enters accidentally." Thus, in order for something to be a characteristic of an object, it has to be a constituent of it; it remains obscure, however, why Erdmann does not also count as constituents and, hence, characteristics of an object "relations into which an object, with all its characteristics, enters accidentally," since he lists relations among characteristics shortly before and shortly afterwards. Furthermore, that the constituents of an object mentioned by Erdmann are not as such to be called characteristics, but only inasmuch as they are presented through corresponding parts of contents, is shown by a remark in which Erdmann, just like Kant, confounds the content with the object of a presentation, but in which he does this, also like Kant, in a fashion which offers a welcome confirmation of our view about characteristics. He says: "The individual constituents of consciousness which are contained in a presentation, the partial presentations, conceived of as determinations of the object, are called "characteristics."[5] The agreement with Kant is complete; hence, what was said there also holds here.

There is no unchangeable boundary between characteristics, that is, between those constituents of an object which are presented through the presentation of this object, and the rest of the constituents of the same object. For example, one can be presented with a table without thinking of the shape of its legs; in this case, the shape of the table legs is a (material, metaphysical) constituent (of second order), but not a characteristic of the table. But if one thinks, while being presented with the table, of the shape of its legs, then the shape has to be considered a characteristic of the table. Experience teaches us that it is

[5] For the above quoted passages see B. Erdmann, *op. cit.*, para. 23.

always a more or less constant stock of constituents of an object which are elevated to characteristics; psychological laws as well as practical needs are responsible for which constituents of an object are represented in the presentation of it; as a rule, they will be, on the one hand, those constituents which are in themselves the most striking ones, on the other hand, those which seem especially suited to distinguish the object in question from certain other objects, or to distinguish it from as many other objects as possible, or to explain a number of other objects, and the like. In order to turn a constituent, of which one assumes that it is usually not presented, into a characteristic, one attaches to the name of the object by means of the word 'as' the name of the respective constituent or group of constituents. Thus one speaks of the circle "as" the limiting case of the ellipse and calls attention, in this manner, to those constituents (properties) of the circle which it shares with that conic section; similarly, when one speaks of Cassius as the murderer of Caesar, of Salzburg as the birthplace of Mozart, of a tree as an organism.

In view of the definition of the characteristic here propounded as a *presented* constituent of the object, one must more than ever guard against the mistake discussed earlier (chapter 8) of thinking of the characteristic as a constituent of the content of a presentation. The temptation to make this mistake is great because of the ambiguity of the expression 'being presented.' It may therefore not be superfluous to point out anew that 'being presented' when attributed to the characteristic must be taken in the determining sense and not in the modifying sense. If the characteristic is said to be a presented constituent, then this does not mean that it is a constituent of the content of a presentation; it remains now, as ever, a constituent of the object. It merely means that this constituent of the object enters into a certain relationship with the conceiving subject in that it is presented to the subject.

Now, all known constituents of every object without exception are capable of being presented; those which cannot be presented in intuition are surely presented in a non-intuitive way. To be sure, not all constituents need therefore be conceivable in the sense that one can pick out any given one whatsoever and conceive of it aside from all other constituents; also, it is impossible to conceive of all, or even of a tolerably large number of constituents, through *one* presentation. The formal constituents of an object are not conceivable if the material constituents, for which the formal constituents are the form of connection, are not conceived of; furthermore, the presentations of different characteristics, be they material or formal constituents, presuppose each other psychologically; thus color presupposes extension, equiangularity presupposes the angles of the triangle. And if the number of constituents of an object is very large, then one cannot help – in the case of an intuitive presentation – but conceive of the object in a discursive fashion, that is, by conceiving of the individual characteristics successively, and by establishing a reference to a uniform object through the presentations of the property relations of the characteristics which all point to one single common term.

But even though the boundary between the constituents of an object which are characteristics and those which are not must in general be called fluid, and even though this boundary varies from one conceiving subject to another, and even, within limits, for the same individual, and the same presentation, some philosophers have nevertheless believed that certain characteristics always recur. We are here not talking tabout constituents which have to be conceived of whenever one conceives of a *particular* object. For, in this case, there can be no question but that, say, three sides always have to be conceived as often as one is intuitively presented with a triangle; that a certain shape always occurs in connection with the presentation of a horse as a characteristic of the horse, and the like. Rather, what is claimed is that certain characteristics belong to all objects of whatever kind, whenever they be conceived and by whomever. Hence, certain constituents supposedly belong to every object, and these constituents are always and necessarily conceived of, so that a presentation is not even possible, unless these constituents are presented by means of it. Sigwart expresses this view as follows: "When we conceive of a certain tone as such, then we can only do so by thinking of it as being *one*, as being self-identical, and as being different from others; only in this way is it an object of our consciousness, which is not at all conceivable without a plurality of distinguished objects. Hence, when we are thinking of the tone *A*, the presentation of *unity* and of the *identity* with itself as well as the difference from others, and hence the presentation of a plurality of these others, is inevitably also posited; and this circumstance refers back to functions through which we posit something as one, self-identical, entity which is distinguished from others, and thereby think of a plurality as distinguished and in relation to a unit. Thus, in calling to mind what we conceive of when we conceive of *A* we find, in addition to the audible tone, also these determinations in the presentation of *A*, and this presentation, as it is present in our consciousness, proves therefore to be a complex product."[6]

It is clear that unity and self-identity as well as difference from other objects are constituents of every object, namely, constituents of a metaphysical nature in the sense mentioned by us in the footnote on page 55. These are in part relations in the object itself and hence formal constituents of it; in part, relations between the object and other objects, hence material constituents of the object. But whether these constituents are also characteristics seems questionable. If through every presentation of an object its difference from all other objects is simultaneously presented, then all of these other objects – which are different from the given one, as Sigwart himself notes – must also be presented. But this is impossible, since with every presentation of an object there would have to occur the presentations of all other objects which are known to the person in question – something nobody would wish to assert. Hence the difference between an object and all other objects is certainly not also presented; this difference is indeed a constituent of every object, but not a characteristic.

But, perhaps, at least that difference is simultaneously presented which obtains between a given object, on the one hand, and those objects, on the other hand, which are most similar to the given object, which are most easily confused with it? Then only a few relations of difference, including their terms, would have to be presented, and the psychological impossibility which stood in the way of the previous assumption would not arise. But here, too, experience teaches us the opposite. It may have to be admitted, in a few cases, that it is possible that the difference between an object and a few others is also presented and that, therefore, these other objects themselves are also presented. This possibility is realized when someone makes the acquaintance of an object which was previously unknown to him, but which is similar to other objects, and when this person now tries to fix its difference from those other objects in his memory. If one conceives of a wolf for the first time, then one will almost automatically compare it with a dog and consider the differences between the two. What causes this comparison here is an association by means of similarity; but one can also resist this association and conceive of a wolf without thinking at all of a dog. No matter how closely we look at the kind of situation under consideration, never, or only very seldom, will we find that we

[6] Sigwart, *op. cit.*, vol. 1, para. 41, 7.

conceive of even a single relation of difference when we have a presentation of an object – not counting, of course, those cases where we conceive of an object with the help of relations in which its stands to others, where we, therefore, conceive of it indirectly.

In regard to self-identity, whose presentation, according to Sigwart, forms a constituent of every presentation of an object, it appears to us that B. Erdmann has already completely and accurately clarified the situation.[7] His considerations culminate in the result that every object is indeed identical with itself and, hence that identity forms a (metaphysical) constituent of every object, but that "the presentation of self-identity is only in exceptional cases contained as a characteristic in the self-identical entity which is presented." "From a logical point of view," Erdmann says, "self-identity is a characteristic which belongs to every object; for, it is found in the object among the logical conditions for analysis, as such it appears as contained in the object. From a psychological point of view, it is missing inasmuch as we, directing our attention to the special nature of the presented object, have no occasion to become conscious of a characteristic which belongs to everything presented, of something which is constant, in addition to what changes, from object to object." Hence we say that identity is a constituent which belongs to every object without exception, but which is only in exceptional cases a characteristic of the objects of presentations.

From the fact that self-identity belongs, as a constituent, to all presented objects without exception, Erdmann deduces the assertion that the basic law of identity expresses "in the essence of the object the most general condition for all presentation possible to us" and that it could, therefore, be called "the basic law of our presentations." "Identity forms the core of what has been called, since Kant, position [*Position*], positing and with an unhappily chosen expression, since it is taken from the area of judgment, affirmation." The two relations, "the basic one of identity and the derived one of non-identity, exhaust the basic relationships of what is presented as such. All the others require a consideration of the special contents of the object, and this is only possible with reference to judgmental relations [*Urteilsbeziehungen*]."

In these last mentioned passages, what is correct seems to be mixed up with what is incorrect. For, it is unquestionably to be admitted that every object is identical with itself and not identical with others. This feature, formulated in one sentence, can therefore also be put

[7] B. Erdmann, *op. cit.*, vol. 1, para. 33.

forward as a law under which every object falls, just as every body falls under the law of attraction. Only, it appears questionable, firstly, whether the mentioned features – self-identity, difference from all other objects – are really the only ones which belong to what is presented as such and, secondly, whether these relationships are the basic ones for all objects of presentations.

In regard to the first question, we have already had occasion to refer to some general features of objects of presentations. We saw that all objects of presentations are, not only conceivable – this follows obviously from the very notion – but also judgeable as well as desirable and abhorrable. These determinations of objects, too, are – what Erdmann wants to allow only for identity and non-identity – independent of the special nature of every single object and belong to everything presented without exception. But one must agree with Erdmann that the mentioned features – perhaps with the exception of the first, namely, conceivability – are not to be counted as basic ones. The situation seems to be quite different for another feature of objects which we have already mentioned, namely, their unity, and a brief consideration will show that, in regard to this feature we must answer the second question negatively.

Everything that is presented as an object, no matter how complex it is, is presented as a unified whole. Its parts are united into this unified whole through property relations which have a common term on one side. If the child at the beginning does not differentiate, as it does later, among the objects surrounding it, and even if it constructs out of all the impressions available to it at a given moment *one* object presentation which it later learns to analyze into relatively simpler ones – if, for example, it conceives in this fashion of the wall with its pictures, the ceiling, and a person in the room as a whole – even though all of this may not agree with the objective situation, nevertheless, the object of the presentation of the child is as such a unified whole. This feature of the object of a presentation, in virtue of which the scholastics called it "*unum,*" is a general one. Furthermore, it is the basis for the non-identity and identity of the object. For, in being one, a unified whole, every object sets itself off against all others, as different from all others, and hence as the one it is, as self-identical.

But this "unity" of the object is not only a property, a constituent, but also a characteristic of all objects. One does not only conceive, through every presentation, of *one* object, but one also conceives of it *as being one.*[8] In the case of a complex object, this unity is presented by means of the property relations; in the case of a simple object or an object which is presented as simple, there is no need for this means. If every object were not presented as *one*, then it would blend into others, and no judgment, no emotion would be conceivable which concerns a definite object. Of course, one might say that under these circumstances one must also conceive of the difference between this object and others. But this is mere appearance, created by the fact that the difference from other objects is a property which follows from the unity of every object; however, not all the properties which follow from a characteristic of an object are simultaneously presented. Otherwise, every time one is presented with a square, the equality of its diagonals would have to be presented. Now, the unity is presented, and since it is therefore not only a feature but also a characteristic of every object of a presentation, it appears to be a better basis for a law about all objects of presentations as such than identity, an identity of which we are only occasionally aware.[9]

The question whether or not there are constituents of objects which not only belong to all objects without exception, but which are also characteristics of all objects, must therefore be answered partly in the sense of Sigwart, partly in the sense of Erdmann. For, on the whole, Erdmann is right when he maintains that, although the constituents mentioned by Sigwart can be shown, through analysis, to belong to every object, they are not presented simultaneously through the presentation of an object. However, in regard to *one* of these constituents, Sigwart seems to be right, namely, in regard to unity. For, we believe that we must assert that it is presented every time one is presented with an object, and hence that it is not only a constituent but also a characteristic of every object.

[8] See below, Chapter 15, in regard to the obvious objection that there are also presentations through which one is presented with several objects.

[9] When Meinong says: "Identity is attributed to something, inasmuch as it stands simultaneously in relation to different things," then this seems to confirm our view, according to which the unity of an object precedes by nature its self-identity. For, the object is self-identical inasmuch as it stands, as a unified whole, in property relations to its constituents. (Meinong, *Hume-Studien* II, in *Sitzungsberichte der phil.-hist. Classe der kaiserl. Akademie der Wissenschaften*, vol. CI (Wien, 1882), VII, para. 2.)

## 14. INDIRECT PRESENTATIONS

We turn now to the second part of the question raised at the beginning of the last chapter. The point is to decide whether there corresponds to every part of the content of a presentation a certain part of the object which is presented through it; while there is general agreement, an agreement seldom found in matters of psychology, about the earlier question, this is not the case for the question which we have to face now. Bolzano, for example, maintains "that there are various constituents of a presentation which do not at all express properties of the object which corresponds to it."[1] Kerry, on the other hand, holds the view "that the object of a concept must *in a certain sense* have at least all the characteristics of its concept; otherwise, one could not say that it falls under the concept."[2] We shall now seek to determine who of the two scholars is right.

As formulated by Bolzano, the principle quoted will certainly have to be accepted. For we know that the content of a presentation can contain constituents to which there correspond, in the object, parts which are not to be called its "properties." This is the case, for example, when the terms of a series are presented. The presentation of the series contains constituents to which there correspond as objects parts of the series, and these parts are most certainly not properties of the series. But Bolzano goes even further and defends the assertion that one cannot say that "every part of a presentation is the presentation of a part of its object."[3] Now, this is undoubtedly correct if one has the formal constituents of a presentation in mind. Since these are not presentations at all, they could not possibly be presentations of any parts of an object. But Bolzano maintains his assertion also

[1] Bolzano, *op. cit.*, para. 64.
[2] Kerry, *op. cit.*, vol. 10, p. 422.
[3] *Op. cit.*, para. 63.

for the material constituents of the content of a presentation and marshals several arguments which have to be tested for their soundness.

According to Bolzano, presentations which contain in their contents more material constituents than their objects have parts are, firstly, presentations which contain as parts whole sentences, for example, the presentation of a triangle "which has a right angle"; secondly, presentations of objects which "since they are perfectly simple, have no parts at all, while their presentations, nevertheless, are quite obviously composed of several parts – every mental being, for example, is a perfectly simple object, although its concept is composed of several parts." Thirdly, presentations of the following kind: "the eye of the human being, the gable of the house." The contents of these presentations contain the presentations of the human being and of the house as constituents; yet the human being is not a part of his eye, the house, not a part of its gable. Rather, the opposite relationship holds between these objects. Bolzano thinks that this kind of presentation is most suited to prove his assertion in an "irrefutable" way. Fourthly, presentations like "a country without mountains," "a book without pictures." "For these presentations do obviously not refer through the constituent presentations *mountain* and *picture* to parts of the objects which fall under them, but rather to those which they lack."

These are Bolzano's arguments to the effect that certain presentations contain material constituents through which no constituents of the objects are presented which fall under them.

Bolzano himself does not attach too much weight to the first of these arguments. For "one concedes willingly that it is in such a case not the whole sentence, but only a presentation occurring in it which refers to a part that can also be found in the object. This is indeed sometimes the case; for example, the presentation of a rectangular triangle, that is, the presentation of a triangle which has a right angle, refers in the sentence 'which has a right angle' to the presentation of a right angle which indeed points to a part of the rectangular triangle." But that this is not always the case will be shown by the examples mentioned in the fourth place.

In regard to the second of Bolzano's arguments, which adduces presentations of simple objects, we have already emphasized that there are no simple objects, that is, objects for which one could not discern relations between them and other objects. When we conceive of a simple object, say, God, then we do so by conceiving of individual relations between this object and other objects, relations which are (metaphysical) parts of the – in *other* respects certainly simple – object. And with this fact in mind, Bolzano's second argument must be dealt with in the same way as his third and fourth arguments; all three arguments concern objects which are presented by means of relations in which they stand to other objects.

Such presentations are called indirect. Kerry describes the form of such presentations in the following way: the object of such a concept is thought of by means of a relation, one term of which is known; the object itself is the other term, and it is through this position (through that relation and its known term) sufficiently determined, provided the relation under consideration is univocal in regard to the unknown and, hence, to be determined term. Since different relations may be involved in situations of this kind, a certain variety of ways of thinking those concepts is the result.[4] All the examples mentioned by Bolzano in the second, third, and fourth of his arguments belong to the kind of presentation here described in Kerry's words.

To be sure, one must not believe that when one conceives in this manner of an object indirectly that then nothing else is ever presented in regard to this object, except that it is something which stands to another object in a certain relation. The presentation *father of Socrates* is certainly an indirect presentation in the sense just explained. The known term is Socrates; the relation is the one in which a son stands to his father; and Sophroniskos is the other term of the relation, the term which is determined by the relation and its one known term. 'Sophroniskos' and 'father of Socrates' both name the same object. But the relationship of fatherhood is such that it can take as terms only male organisms, and the known term of this relation, Socrates, excludes the presentation of all organisms with the exception of human beings. Hence, what one is presented with through that indirect presentation is not absolutely "an *object* which stands to Socrates in the relation of fatherhood," but rather: "a *man* who, etc." However, in some cases the relation does not determine the kind of objects which are related to a given one; the indirect presentation is then to a larger or smaller degree indeterminate; for example, the presentation of something which is in my possession. Therefore, the univocacy of the relation emphasized by Kerry is not a necessary condition for indirect presentations.

Bolzano's examples stand in the middle between these two kinds of indirect presentations, the determinate and the indeterminate kinds.

[4] Kerry, *op. cit.*, vol. 9, p. 461.

The eye which stands to the human being in the relation of part to whole, the country which stands to mountains in the relation called "lack or absence of something," these objects are – to use a phrase of Erdmann's – only indeterminately determined objects. They are determined as to kind, but not as to individual.

Now, the question arises whether these indirect presentations are such, as Bolzano will have it, that they contain material constituents through which *no* parts of the objects of these presentations are presented. Bolzano's arguments are prepossessing. Whoever conceives of a human eye, certainly also conceives of a human being; and yet a human being is not part of his eye. And whoever is presented with a country without mountains, is certainly also presented with mountains, and yet mountains are not part of a country which is characterized as having no mountains. Now, one could try to find a way out by saying that one conceives through such presentations of several objects, not just of one, and that the objects presented are a relation and its two terms. Whoever conceives of a country without mountains, conceives of (1) a country, (2) mountains, (3) a relation between these two objects, namely, a relation according to which the latter has to be denied of the former. But this way out proves to be impossible, too, if one recalls our description of what one has to understand by the object of a presentation. According to that description (chapter 7), the object of a presentation is what is designated by the name which means the content of the presentation, it is that which is – on the basis of this mental content – judged, desired or abhorred. The first of these criteria may at first appear to be fulfilled. For, the complex name 'eye of the human being' does indeed designate the eye, the human being, while by means of the addition in *casu obliquo* of the second name to the first, one expresses the relation between both objects. But there must be a difference between this complex name and the separate mention of every one of its constituents as a name standing by itself. And that the mentioned names do not form a simple concatination of three names emerges from the following consideration.

If the object of the presentation of the country without mountains were a complex consisting of the country, the mountains, and a relation between the two, then this complex would have to be what a judgment concerning the country without mountains is about, it would have to be what is desired or abhorred in an emotion which is directed toward it. But this is obviously not the case. If someone says that he loves a country without mountains, then he does not say thereby that he loves *mountains*; and when someone makes a judgment about the human eye, then his judgment concerns only the *eye* of the human being, not also the human being. But if the latter belonged to the complex designated by 'the human eye,' then it, too, would have to be involved in the judgment. If someone then said that there is no country in which there exists any wooden iron, which is obviously a true judgment, he would also be asserting the existence of wooden iron. Hence it is equally not the case that, through the presentation of the human eye or the presentation of a country without mountains, these objects occur in some kind of connection. The assumption that in this case *one* content corresponds to several objects proves untenable.

And we are once again faced with the fact that if one names the human eye, one conceives of a human being, while, at the same time, the human being cannot belong to the mentioned object; for, otherwise, it would have to be judged, desired, or abhorred together with that object. All the same, we must not give in to Bolzano's arguments because they rest on a confusion between the content of a presentation – and hence the meaning of the name for this presentation – and the auxiliary presentations [*Hilfsvorstellungen*] which are related to the so-called inner speech form [*Sprachform*], the *etymon*. As soon as we keep these two things strictly apart, it turns out that indirect presentations also do not contain in their contents a single material constituent through which no part of their objects is presented.

As is well known, one speaks of an inner speech form whenever there is directly attached to a perceptible sign – for example, a noise – a presentation "which is not meant, but which merely serves to mediate the meaning. It is not the entity designated, but itself a sign just like the noise."[5] This presentation which is directly attached to the noise is called "the inner speech form." When the presentations of a plow and its use were attached to the name 'earth,' at a time when every speaker was conscious of its etymon, these presentations were then as little as they are now the meaning of the name. They merely served to evoke the presentation of the object to which the plow is applied and were, therefore, really nothing else but signs which aroused the respective content of a presentation; just as it is today the name 'earth' alone which awakens that content without any mediation by auxiliary presentations.

[5] Marty, *Ueber das Verhaeltnis von Logik und Grammatik*, p. 106.

The presentation of a human being serves the same purpose in regard to the presentation of the human eye as the etymon in regard to the presentation which is associated with it, which is the true meaning of the respective name. Let us hear what Marty has to say about this: "Inasmuch as presentations of the inner form ... merely facilitate the understanding, ... one can compare them, not inappropriately, with circumlocutory [*umschreibende*] definitions. These, too, do not *directly* give the meaning of the name which is to be defined, but arouse first of all certain auxiliary presentations which may lead to the meaning, and they are, therefore, like riddles, except that they are not supposed to be difficult, but rather are supposed to yield with the greatest possible ease the correct solution. The circumlocutory definition names sometimes a *proprium* of the respective concept; sometimes, its genus; sometimes, its species; sometimes, examples of it; it points at unambiguous analogies or contrasts; it gives causes or the effects of the intended objects; or it mentions some other fixed *correlate* of the object; often, however, it merely points at an accidental *relation* which provides the desired clue for the listener only because of the special context that happens to prevail. Such would be the case, for example, if someone explained the sense of the name of a color by pointing out that this color happens to be the color of a piece of furniture or apparel in the vicinity."[6]

We have italicized in this quotation what, for our purposes, is most important. The solution to Bolzano's arguments emerges, therefore, as follows: Whoever uses the name 'country without mountains,' arouses by means of it in the listener the presentation of mountains, the presentation of a judgment which denies the mountains of a country, and the presentation of a country. The first two presentations are auxiliary presentations designed to call up the presentation of a country of a certain kind. The presentation of this country is the true meaning of the name 'country without mountains'; whatever else in the way of presentations may occur in the listener does not belong to the meaning of this name, but merely helps to make this meaning conscious. That the task of these auxiliary presentations is indeed the same as that of names, and that it consists in arousing the meant content in the listener, follows further from the fact that the name 'country without mountains' can be replaced by another one, say, 'flat country,' in which the function formerly distributed between

[6] *Op. cit.*, p. 112.

linguistic signs and auxiliary presentations is now played by the linguistic signs alone. What is meant by the two names, the content of the presentations aroused by them, is the same, just as what is designated is in both cases the same object.

In general, for indirect presentations, the situation is as follows: Every indirectly presented content comes about through the intermediary of auxiliary presentations. These are – recall Kerry's description of indirect presentations – the presentation of the known term of the relation and, in part, also the presentation of this relation. For, this relation is a part of the presentation of the known term as well as of the unknown, indirectly presented, term. In regard to the former, it is a part of the auxiliary presentation; in regard to the latter, it belongs as a material constituent to the actually meant content. Now, through the auxiliary presentation, too, one is certainly presented with an object; but just as the presentation of this object is not *meant* by the name which means the indirect presentation, so the object is also not designated by the name.

Since all the examples adduced by Bolzano in defense of his view are indirect presentations, they do not prove what they are supposed to prove. For, the presentation of the human being is *not* a part of the presentation of the human eye, but is an auxiliary presentation, to be sharply distinguished from the former, which, as a sign, arouses the really meant presentation, namely, that of an eye of a certain kind. The relation which obtains here between the known term and the unknown term is that of whole to part. If we had a name for the eye of the human being which does not mention the human being, then it would be even more apparent that the presentation of a human being is not a constituent of the presentation of the human eye. Compare the example mentioned above: Sophroniskos = father of Socrates.

The same holds for the presentation of the country without mountains. The relation between the known term and the unknown term is here that of lacking, that is, a relation which obtains between two objects if one has to be denied of the other. Among the auxiliary presentations which arouse an indirect presentation of this kind there is, therefore, always the presentation of a double judgment [*Doppelurteil*].[7] Such auxiliary presentations can be shown for all so-called

[7] By double judgments – in distinctions to simple ones – we understand those which do not only affirm or deny an object, but which also ascribe something to it or deny something of it. Compare Hillebrand, *op. cit.*, paras. 67 ff.

negative presentations; such presentations form a class of indirect presentations.

Thus we see that the indirect presentations do not contain material constituents through which no parts of the corresponding objects are presented. In addition to the three groups of material constituents of the content of a presentation through which one is presented, respectively, with the material constituents of an object and its primary and secondary formal constituents (of course, not with their totality), there exist no other material constituents of the content of a presentation.

Before we close this chapter, we want to consider the question of what relationship there is between the presentation of an object and the presentation of the presentation of this object. Kerry investigated this question for logical and epistemological purposes and he arrived at the result that the presentation of a presentation is equal to this presentation itself.[8] He says: "The concept of a concept is a complex concept whose closer parts are: the general relation between concept and object (a), and the concept itself (b). It is immediately clear that an understanding of the constituent (b) is equivalent to a knowledge of the object of the concept: (b) is simply the object of the concept under consideration .... Indeed, the concept of a concept does not add anything new to the primary concept, but is merely a copy of the primary concept; the concept of a concept is equal to the concept itself .... By the way, the function mentioned here is strictly analogous, if you will, to the infinitely continuing chain of affirmations of the same judgmental content: the affirmation of an affirmation is equal to the affirmation itself."

We must here separate truth from falsehood. If we call the object which is presented $G$, the content of the presentation of this object $I$, and the content of the presentation of $I$ is called $I'$, then a comparison between $I$ and $I'$ shows the following: the material constituents of $I$ are presentations of the constituents of $G$. However, in addition to these material constituents, $I$ also contains formal constituent. Now, if one conceives of $I$ itself, then this is the object ($G' = I$) of the presentation whose content is called $I'$. The material constituents of $I'$ are presentations of material and formal constituents of $I$. Some of the material constituents of $I'$ have as an object the material constituents of $I$; these, in turn, have as an object the material and

[8] Kerry, *op. cit.*, vol. 10, p. 458 f.

formal constituents of $G$. Other material constituents of $I'$ have as an object the formal constituents of $I$, but these have nothing else as object, since they are not presentations at all. Hence the presentation of a presentation adds something new to the primary presentation inasmuch as through $I'$ also the formal constituents of $I$ are presented; on the other hand, one can call $I'$ a copy of $I$, since through $I'$ no constituent of $G$ comes to be conceived of which is not already conceived of through $I$, that is, through the primary presentation. *As far as knowledge of the object of the concept is concerned,* therefore, the presentation of the presentation of the object is equivalent to the primary presentation of the object; in an absolute sense, though, $I$ and $I'$ are not only different from each other because of a difference in constituents, but also because of the fact that the object of $I'$ is a presentation, $I = G'$, while the object of $I$ is $G$.

The analogy from the field of judgmental activity, which Kerry draws for his view, agrees precisely with our account of the relationship between a presentation and the presentation of this presentation. For, if one affirms the affirmation of an object, then one affirms thereby, *in regard to the object,* nothing more than what one affirms by means of the primary affirmation itself. Hence, the second affirmation is equivalent to the first in all logical respects insofar as the object of the original affirmation is concerned. But there is a difference between the two affirmations, since by means of the second affirmation one affirms implicitly, not only the object of the first affirmation, but also this affirmation itself. Similarly, as we have seen, through the presentation $I'$ one is not only presented with constituents of the object $G$, mediated by the material constituents of the presentation $I$, but one is also presented simultaneously with formal constituents of the content $I$. To the latter, there corresponds in the analogy as the relevant phenomenon the primary affirmation; to the former, the mediately presented constituents of $G$, there corresponds the object which is already affirmed through the primary affirmation.

## 15. THE OBJECTS OF GENERAL PRESENTATIONS

Earlier, we mentioned an argument (chapter 6, 4) that is used by Kerry to demonstrate a difference between the content and the object of a presentation. We remarked then that we cannot use this argument for reasons which will have to be explained later. This argument is based on the assertion that several objects belong to a general concept and that, therefore, the content of a presentation cannot be identified with its object.[1] We must now explain the reason why we have said that it is inadmissible to rely on this argument of Kerry's.

The reason is no other than that there are no presentations to which a plurality of objects belong. It is true that the opposite is generally assumed. Bolzano even asserts that nobody has ever denied that there are presentations which are related to an infinite number of objects.[2] Now, even though there have been many logicians since Bolzano, one will search in vain for an explicit assertion by any of them to the effect that there exist no presentations to which there correspond a plurality of objects. We shall try to show in what follows that the situation is nevertheless what we have just maintained it is.

If there is a presentation to which there corresponds a plurality of objects, then these objects must be countable, at least, when their number is finite. It is actually believed that one can count the objects of such presentations. It is this belief which is mistaken. For, what one counts are not the objects which are intended by the respective general presentation, but objects of as many other presentations as the objects one happens to be counting. Consider the process of counting objects. If I want to count, say, the pictures which hang in this room, then there appears, first of all, in my consciousness the general presentation of *picture which hangs in this room*. But with the help of this general presentation alone I cannot as yet count. If I want to

[1] Kerry, *op. cit.*, vol. 10, p. 432.
[2] Bolzano, *op. cit.*, para. 68.

start counting, then it becomes necessary to conceive of the individual pictures themselves. And only by doing this – thus conceiving of every picture as different from the others, and taking care that no picture conceived of for the purpose of counting is conceived of for a second time for the same purpose – can I carry out the counting. Nobody, by the way, seems to deny this, namely, that in order to be able to count those objects which are united into some "higher" unit, one has to have the presentations of these individual objects themselves.

But, it may be objected, the objects whose individual presentations one has to have in order to be able to count them, are at the same time the objects of a presentation which is superordinated to all of these individual presentations; they are objects of the respective general presentation. It is just the peculiarity of the general presentation that it puts before our mind in one fell swoop a plurality of objects, each of which can be presented through one or several presentations.

This last assertion cannot mean that the general presentation does precisely what the individual presentations, taken together, do. If, on the one hand, one conceives successively of a number of objects – which belong to a natural or an artificial genus – through the corresponding individual presentations and, on the other hand, has the respective general presentation itself, then this general presentation accomplishes something quite different – as no one denies – from what those individual presentations accomplish when combined. This follows, among other things, from the fact that one can have a general presentation also in those cases where the number of objects of the corresponding individual presentations, and hence these presentations themselves, is infinitely large. For example, if the general presentation of number were nothing else but a collection of all the individual presentations of all individual numbers, then the peculiar properties of individual numbers would have to be just as specifiable when one merely has the general presentation of number as when one has the individual presentations of all the individual numbers. Now, this is obviously not the case, and in this respect the general presentation of number accomplishes less than all the individual presentations – which, by the way, are never attainable in their totality – of individual numbers. In another respect, however, the general presentation accomplishes more than the individual presentations which are subsumed under it. For, it makes judgments possible which, in turn, accomplish more than what the individual judgments about the successively presented objects can achieve in their totality. The judgment

*The sum of the inner angles of all triangles, or of the triangle as such is 180°* has a logical value which is quite different from that of the judgment *The sum of the inner angles of triangle A is 180°*, *The sum of the inner angles of triangle B is 180°*, etc., taken together. A judgment arrived at in this fashion by complete induction – which is in this case impossible – does not have the validity of a judgment which is based on the general presentation of the triangle. And is not the fact that one makes the judgment *The sum of the inner angles of all triangles is 180°* with evidence, even though a complete induction is impossible, proof that the general presentation of the triangle yields more than all the individual presentations of the individual triangles combined?

But if the general presentation is different from a summation formula for a finite or infinite series of individual presentations, in what then consists its peculiarity? It consists, one says, in the fact that, by means of it, one conceives of *what is common* as such to all objects of individual presentations. If one admits this, as one surely must, then one concedes also that the object of a general presentation is different from the objects of the individual presentations which are subsumed under it. Now, one could object that one conceives of those constituents which an object shares with other objects even when one conceives of the individual object, but that one pays no attention to the fact that these constituents belong to this object as well as to the others. Accordingly, the general presentation differs from the individual presentations which are subsumed under it only in that through the former one conceives, in addition to a characteristic, also of a certain relation between certain constituents of the object and certain constituents of other objects, namely, the common possession of these constituents. The object of the general presentation of the triangle, therefore, is no other than the object of any arbitrary individual presentation of the same object; only, by means of the former, a relation between certain parts of the object and certain parts of similar objects is presented, while this is not the case for the latter. Thus a general presentation of the triangle is to an individual presentation of an individual triangle what, say, the presentation of Plato as the teacher of Aristotle is to the presentation of Plato absolutely. Through the former, one conceives simultaneously of a certain relationship between Plato and another object; through the latter, one conceives of Plato without being conscious of his relation to Aristotle. This analogy seems to be unobjectionable and fitting; yet it is mistaken. In truth, this analogy does not hold at all. About the object of the presentation of Plato as teacher of Aristotle, one can assert everything that holds for the object of the presentation of Plato absolutely. One can say of the former as well as of the latter that he was born during the eighty-eighth Olympiade, that he was originally called Aristokles, that he composed dialogues, that he taught in the Academy, etc. But if one has a general presentation of the triangle, then one cannot assert about its object the same things which one can assert about the object of an individual presentation of a certain triangle. One can say about the latter that it has an area of about two square inches, a right angle and two acute angles, etc. All of these assertions, however, do not hold for the object of the general presentation of the triangle. One cannot say that the triangle has an area of two square inches, a right angle and two acute angles, etc. For, the general presentation of a triangle is neither the presentation of a rectangular triangle, nor that of a triangle with a certain area. Now, if one has two presentations such that the same judgments hold for both of their objects, then these presentations are equivalent and there is, in truth, only one object. But if one has two presentations, no matter how similar they may be in regard to their contents, such that the same judgements do not hold for their objects, then these objects are different from each other. Since this is the case for the general presentation as compared to the individual presentation, we must proclaim that the object of the general presentation is different from the object of any individual presentation which is subsumed under it.

Therefore, what is presented through a general presentation is a group of constituents which are common to several objects. This group of constituents is presented as a whole that belongs together; this is the object of the general presentation. It is a little admissible to identify this object with the object of the individual presentation as it is to identify, say, the the number ten with the number one hundred (taken as the object of a presentation), even though the presentation of the number ten is contained in the presentation of the number one hundred. The object of the general presentation is a part of the object of a subsumed presentation, a part which stands in the relation of equality to certain parts of objects of other individual presentations.

The general presentation is always indirect and non-intuitive; it is non-intuitive to such a degree that many consider it to be unattainable and deny its existence, just as they deny the existence of presentations whose objects have contradictory characteristics. That such presentations nevertheless exist must be admitted if one acknowledges that one can assert something about their objects. And this is obviously the case. Nobody can intuitively conceive of a "general" triangle; a triangle which is neither right-angled, nor acute-angled, nor obtuse-angled, and which has no color and no determinate size; but there exists an indirect presentation of such a triangle as certainly as there exist indirect presentations of a white horse that is black, of a wooden cannon made of steel, and the like.

That a general presentation has an object which is different from the objects of the individual presentations which are subsumed under it is not a new view. Plato's ideas are nothing else but objects of general presentations. Plato attributes existence to these objects. Today, we do not do so any more; the object of the general presentation is presented to us, but it does not exist; and one can say, at most, that it exists in the sense that it can be found in the objects of the corresponding individual presentations in a form which is modified by the individual characteristics of these individual presentations. It is really amazing that the object of the general presentation, which used to be acknowledged, is nowadays so often overlooked, and that one does not speak of a special object corresponding to the general presentation as such, but replaces it without further ado by the objects of the subsumed individual presentations. We must now try to uncover the probable causes for this mistake. If we succeed, then we shall have gained some support for the view here maintained. Let us note, before we start, that for reasons of simplifying the terminology, we shall speak of general and individual objects instead of objects of general and individual presentations, thus agreeing with Erdmann who thinks that this terminology is the more precise one.[3]

The reason why the general object is so often overlooked seems to be twofold; and it seems to be due, in part, to linguistic, in part, to psychological circumstances. Language often uses the same name as the designation for the general object as well as for the corresponding individual objects. That the names of the individual objects *can* also be different from the name of the general object is shown by the fact that there are proper names. Even if no genuine proper names are available, the names of the individual objects are often different from those of the general objects. In languages which have retained the definite article, the substantive in connection with the definite article

[3] B. Erdmann, *op. cit.*, para. 17. To the best of my knowledge, Erdmann is the only contemporary scholar who acknowledges the general presentation in the sense here defended.

is the genuine name for the general object; in languages which have lost the definite article, its name is the substantive without an addition. When it is a matter of designating an individual object, one uses not infrequently a complex expression composed of the substantive, which designates the corresponding general object, and some further addition to it. Depending on the circumstances, this addition is either a demonstrative pronoun, or a so-called indefinite pronoun (someone, a certain, etc.), or a subordinate clause which mentions individuating characteristics of the object, or the like.

In any case, there is often a similarity between the names of the general objects and those of the corresponding individual objects – if they are not identical to each other – which seems sufficient to explain the fact that one has assumed, taking the mentioned objects as being identical, that a general name is, as it were, the summary designation of all objects which are designated singly be means of the corresponding individual names. This seems to uncover one of the probable reasons for the neglect of general objects.

The other reason consists in the psychological relationship between the presentation of a general object and the presentation of individual objects. There exists a psychological law – already advanced by Aristotle – that one can never have a non-intuitive presentation unless it is accompanied by one (or several) intuitive ones. Whoever has a presentation of the number 1000, does not think of this number – of which he can never have an intuitive picture – without the intuitive presentation of another object which stands to this number in a certain relation. In regard to non-intuitive presentations of numbers, it is usually the written sign, the numeral, that is presented intuitively together with its relation to the number; this relation obtains between the object of the intuitive presentation, the numeral, and the object of the non-intuitive presentation, the number, and is the relation of sign to thing designated. (On this relationship rests the kind of thinking which Leibniz calls "symbolic.") Something similar happens in connection with non-intuitive presentations which are as highly non-intuitive as, say, the presentation of a white horse that is black. This presentation is either restricted to a mere symbolic thinking (in the sense of Leibniz) of the object by means of the name which designates it, or it uses the intuitive presentation of a black horse and transforms the object of this presentation by means of a simultaneous presentation of a negative judgment (the black horse is not black) and a positive judgment (the black horse is white) – both of which are false and conceived of as such (hence, the so-called "unattainability" of such presentations) – into the object of the presentation of a white horse which is black. Now, the way in which general objects are presented is the same as that mentioned earlier for indirect presentations. A general object can only be presented in an indirect way. Its presentation requires an intuitive auxiliary presentation. This is a presentation which is subsumed under the presentation of the general object. Whoever conceives of man in general cannot do so – again, unless this presentation is merely symbolic – without conceiving of an individual man. And here, too, presentations of judgments play the role of mediator between the presentation of the individual man and that of man in general. These presented judgments concern the particular size, color of skin, in short, everything that when combined constitutes the *individuality* of the individual man. But this individuality is not really denied – the judgments are only presented in the modifying sense of the word – but is merely presented as denied. Since not just one, but several – often, even infinitely many – individual presentations are equally suited to bring about the non-intuitive presentation of the general object, and since one may, therefore, be conscious of a whole series of individual objects while conceiving of a single general object, and since, furthermore, the presentations of these individual objects, being intuitive, have a greater vivacity than the non-intuitive general presentation, therefore it may easily appear as if the individual objects of the psychologically dependent auxiliary presentations are in reality what is presented through the general presentation which, compared with each of these auxiliary presentations, is kept constant. But just as the object of the presentation of the number 1000 is different from the object of the contributing auxiliary presentation of the numeral which designates this number, just as furthermore, the object of the presentation of the white horse which is black is different from the object of the presentation of the black horse which occurs simultaneously, so also is the object of the general presentation different from the object of the individual presentation which makes that presentation possible; or, in case several such individual presentations occur successively, it is different from the objects which correspond to these presentations. Only because one has overlooked this fact could one hold that these individual objects are presented through the general presentation which is superordinated to its individual presentations; and this is the psychological cause of the mistake which consists in ascribing several, even infinitely many, objects to a general presentation.

What is presented through the general presentation is an object which is specifically peculiar to it. The objects of the presentations which are subsumed under this general presentation are not presented through the general presentation, but rather through the individual presentations which accompany it as auxiliary presentations; their number is not definite and can be greater or smaller, depending on the conditions of the general presentation itself and of the conceiving subject, but may never fall below one. This simultaneous excitement of individual presentations through names which mean general presentations is the meaning of the Kantian view that the concept (= general presentation) is related *mediately*, by means of a characteristic which can be common to several things, to the object, while intuition (= individual presentation) is *immediately* related to the object.[4] In a similar vein A. Riehl says: "Contrasted with intuition as an immediate presentation of an object is the concept as its *mediate* presentation, as a presentation of the object through other presentations or through a part of the intuitive total presentation."[5] According to what we have said, the objects of subsumed individual presentations are mediately presented through a general presentation insofar as the presentation of a general object depends on one or more presentations of individual objects. However, this mediate presentation of the individual objects through the corresponding general presentation must be understood very much *cum grano salis*, since, to be exact, through the general presentation itself only the general object is presented, while the individual objects are presented through their own presentations which must accompany the general presentation only because of psychological laws. And one can well imagine a more perfect mental organization than the human being's which would be capable of thinking of general objects without recourse to presentations of the corresponding individual objects.

However, the general presentation can truly be called a mediate presentation in the sense in which all indirect presentations are mediate. They require, in order to be awakened, other presentations, the auxiliary presentations; and these are, like the names which mean general presentations, a means – comparable to the inner speech form – which awakens the general presentation. Hence, general presentations, although they are not mediate presentations of *objects*, are to a higher

[4] *Kritik der reinen Vernunft*, ed. by Kehrbach, p. 278; compare also p. 48.
[5] A. Riehl, "Beitraege zur Logik," *Vierteljahrsschrift fuer wissenschaftliche Philosophie*, vol. 16, p. 7.

degree mediately *awakened* presentations than those whose awakening does not require special auxiliary presentations.

What we said about the relationship between a general presentation and the corresponding individual presentations explains now the similarity between the name which means a general presentation and the name which means individual presentations, a similarity which in many cases increases to complete equality. We seem to be forced to assume that all names, whenever they are used for the first time, are names of intuitive, directly presented objects.[6] The word 'sea' is thus first of all the name of a certain sea. Now, as soon as the necessity arises to designate general objects, the name which originally means the individual presentation will also have to be used, since general presentations can only be awakened by means of auxiliary presentations, so that this name becomes associated with the general object and thus awakens mediately the general presentation. We do indeed find in most names which mean indirect presentations the names through which the auxiliary presentations are called up. Think of the examples cited from Bolzano: eye of the *human being*, country without *mountains*, and the like. The closer the association is, that is, the more constant the relationship is between the auxiliary presentation and the intended presentation, the true meaning of the name, the smaller will be the difference between the name of a presentation when the presentation occurs as its meaning and the name which awakens another presentation by means of that presentation as an auxiliary presentation. Between the individual objects, on the one hand, and the general objects which are superordinated to them, on the other, there always exists the same relationship of subordination or superordination, respectively; a relationship which, in the last analysis, depends on the fact that the general object is in a certain way a metaphysical constituent of the individual objects which are subsumed under it. This fact explains the kinship between the names for both kinds of objects.

If we have succeeded in showing that so-called general presentations, too, have only one object, an object which is different from the objects of the individual presentations subsumed under the general presentation, then the assertions made in this investigation do not require a qualification with regard to general presentations and indirect presentations. They hold, without exception, assuming that they are correct, for all presentations of whatever kind.

[6] Sigwart, *op. cit.*, vol. 1, para. 7, 7.

GPSR Compliance

*The European Union's (EU) General Product Safety Regulation (GPSR) is a set of rules that requires consumer products to be safe and our obligations to ensure this.*

*If you have any concerns about our products, you can contact us on ProductSafety@springernature.com*

In case Publisher is established outside the EU, the EU authorized representative is:

Springer Nature Customer Service Center GmbH
Europaplatz 3
69115 Heidelberg, Germany

**Batch number: 10823775**

Printed by Printforce, the Netherlands